Subway Stories

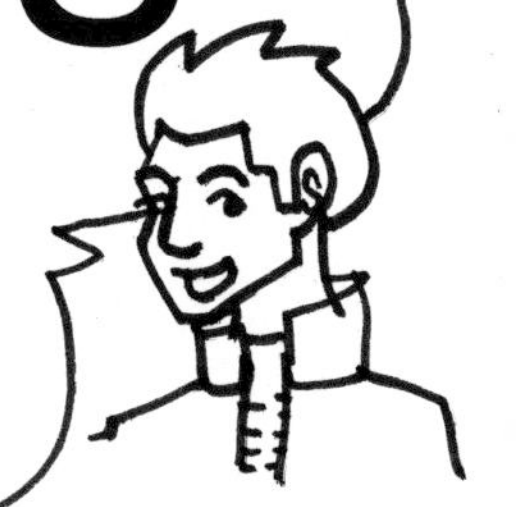

Written by: Apostolos Anagnostopoulos

Illustrated and Designed by: Sophocles Plokamakis

Edited by: Apostolos Plokamakis

A Probato Publication

www.probato.com

978-0692239063

New York

Special Thanks

We would like to thank Apostolos Plokamakis for his tireless help and support in helping us complete Subway Stories. We could not have done it without your patience and dedication. Here's to a great editor!

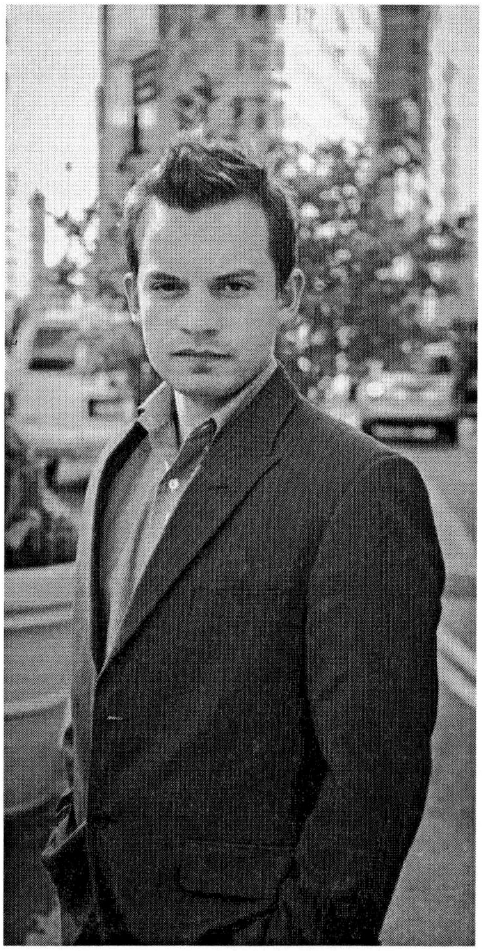

We would like to dedicate this book to New York City commuters who love this city as much as we do!

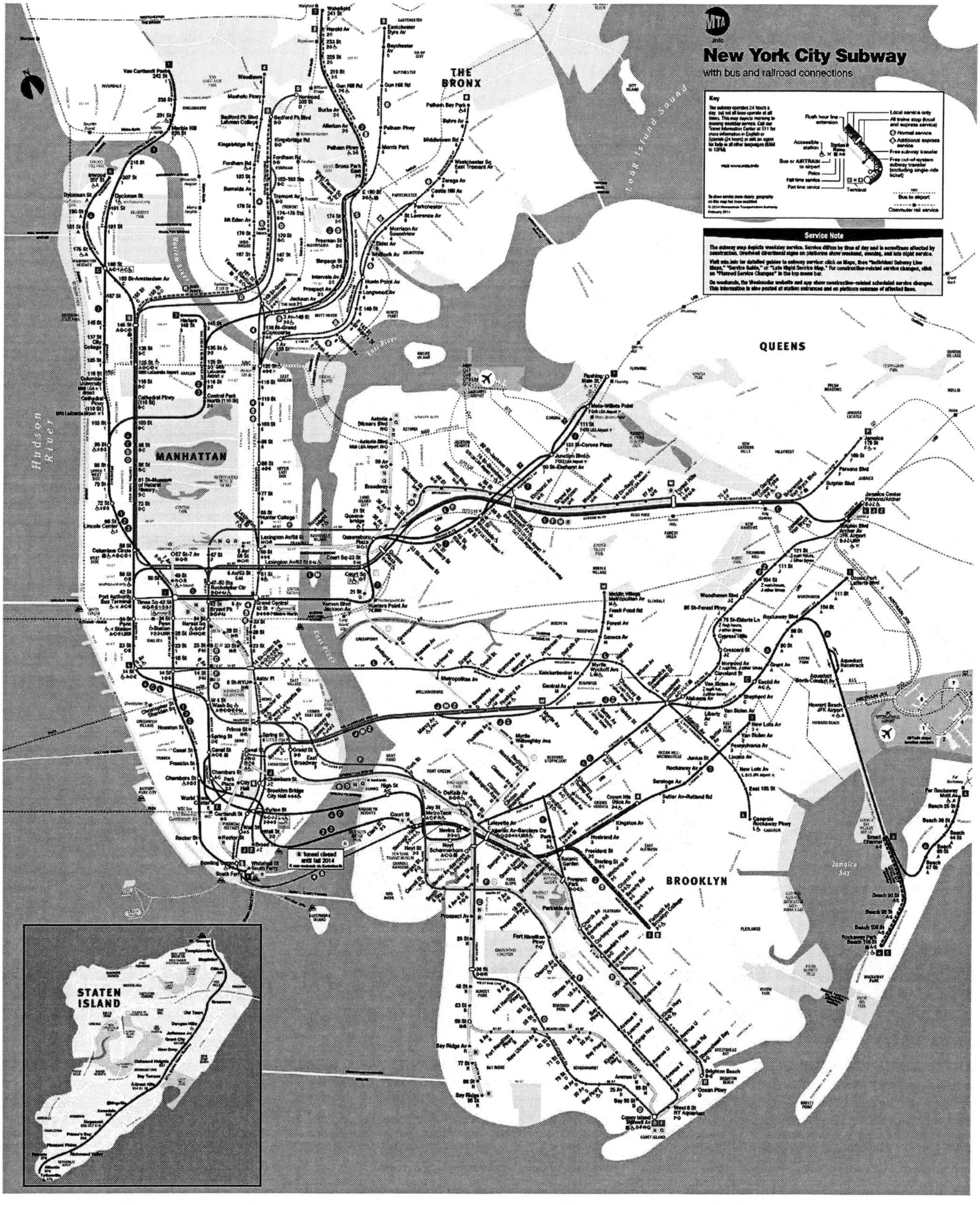

The Story Behind Subway Stories

Note From The Author:

Approximately six months ago, I was first approached by Sophocles to collaborate on a Subway Stories Sketchbook. Sophocles has been sketching every day commuters for the past 3 years; during which time he has closely observed every day occurrences that transpire in the New York City Subway system.

While Sophocles' Subway Sketches paint a picture for viewers to imagine the narrative of the commuters he was drawing, he was repeatedly told that something was missing. His fans wanted to know more about who these people were and what they may be thinking. My collection of subway poems aim to do just that: help guide the reader on a journey about viewing everyday people, places and things in the Subway system with a brand new perspective.

For four months I followed Sophocles through the Subway on most of the trains throughout New York. Although I have traveled through the Subway system before, I knew that I needed to do the proper research. I observed my surroundings in a new light in order to convincingly convey a new but familiar message about the Subway system. After composing several drafts and receiving feedback from my friends, family as well as my editor, Apostolos Plokamakis, I had finally compiled a collection of contemplative, edgy and well written stories about the Subway.

"Subway Stories" marks the second collaboration between comic book artist, Sophocles Plokamakis and I. The first illustrated poetry book we worked on is called Passions of a Poet: Vol. 2: Against All Odds.

I'd like to thank everyone who contributed to the making of Subway Stories and thank the readers for continuing to inspire us to express ourselves. We certainly hope you enjoy our Subway Stories collection!

Note From The Illustrator:

The inspiration for "Subway Stories" was fueled purely by my fascination for the New York City Subway system as well as the commuters that rush in and out each and every day.

The Subway is my studio! I have been sketching on the Subway ever since I began to commute to the School of Visual Arts from Astoria, Queens. Over three years, I have collected hundreds of Subway Sketches, Storyboards, Sumi-e. Over time, I began to create comics in the Subway which I call, Metro Manga. For me every train ride is a new Metro Manga adventure! I have traveled through every stop on all the Subway lines in New York and I have created a Subway Sketch and Metro Manga page on each and every one.

I had the time of my life sharing my passion for the Subway with my older cousin and best friend, Apostolos Anagnostopoulos. It has been a long journey and I have really enjoyed seeing him breathe life into the characters I have created in the great museum and maze that is the Subway!

Thank you for reading our book. We hope you enjoy the journey!

Sincerely, Apostolos and Sophocles

Table of Contents

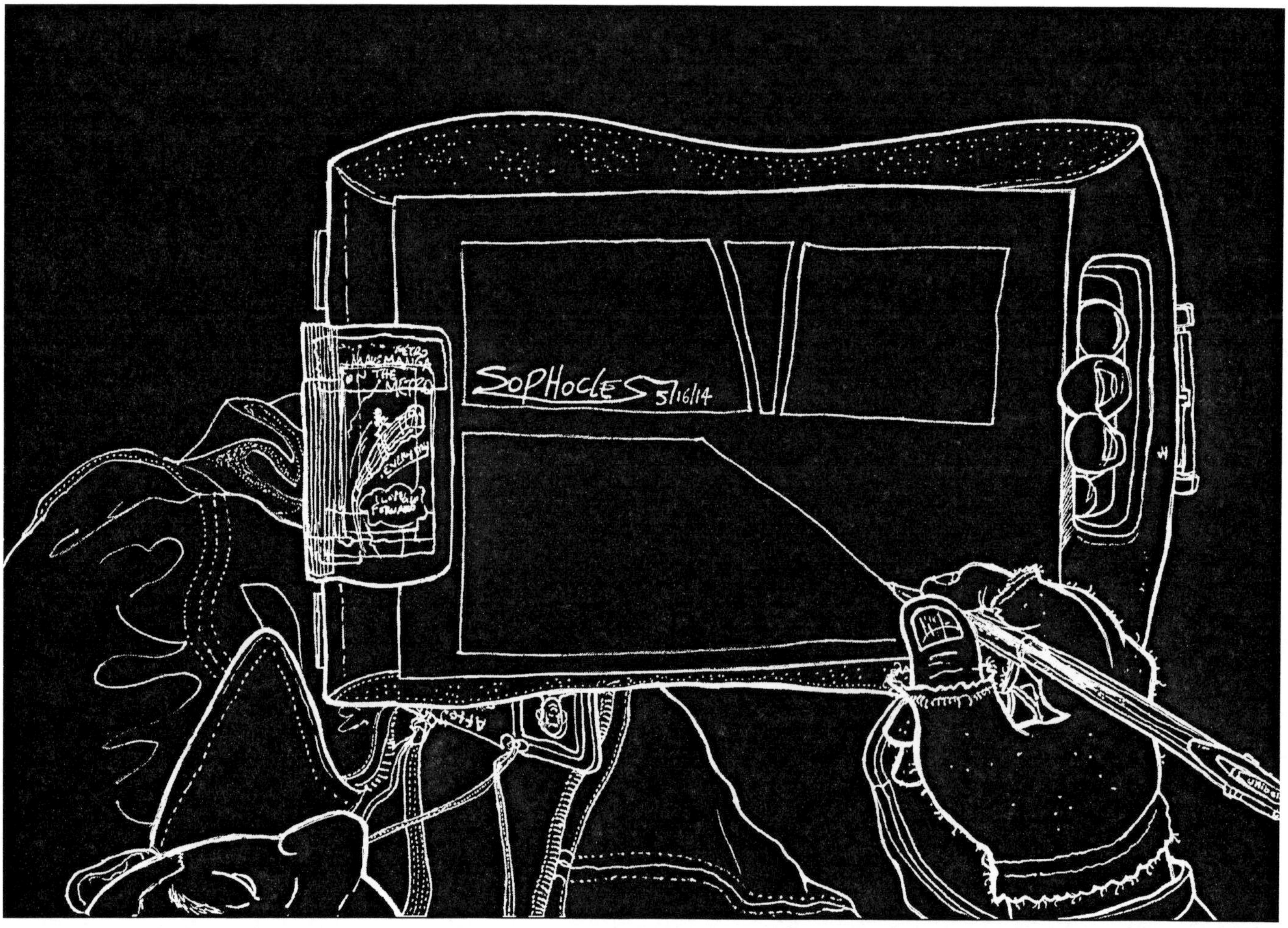
SOPHOCLES 5/16/14

Every Drawing Needs A Drawing Pad

Oh it's 2:10 pm got to rush!
Have to catch the Subway
Students are waiting
To be taught by an artist

Oh there he goes drawing again
How rude of me, let me introduce myself
I'm Sophocles' drawing pad
We roam the Subway together

It is exhilarating, I tell you!
Musicians inspire him
Roaming the Subway stations
Filled with hope and talent
Offering songs to those
Who travel these tunnels

It's quite the rush
To see the expressions
Of the hundreds of passengers
Which pass me by

When the pen brushes across the page
Clipped to my body
I can't help but get excited!
A tingling sensation
Courses through my plastic exterior
I stand firm
Proud to serve as the foundation
Providing the support for him to lean upon
When fashioning his latest masterpiece

Even still…
My importance remains below the surface
Children run up to my owner
Reaching out with their curious hands
Wishing to gaze upon some artistic design

It's hard for people
To look beneath the surface
To see the important things…
What's really keeping it all together
The life of a drawing pad
Lonely at times, yet highly important

If you take anything away
From my worn out ramblings
Please hold on to this:
It is easy to become captivated
By the smooth shiny surface,
A bold design or a new artistic expression
Remember though
Every pen needs ink
Every paper needs a pen
And every drawing…
Well, every drawing needs a drawing pad!

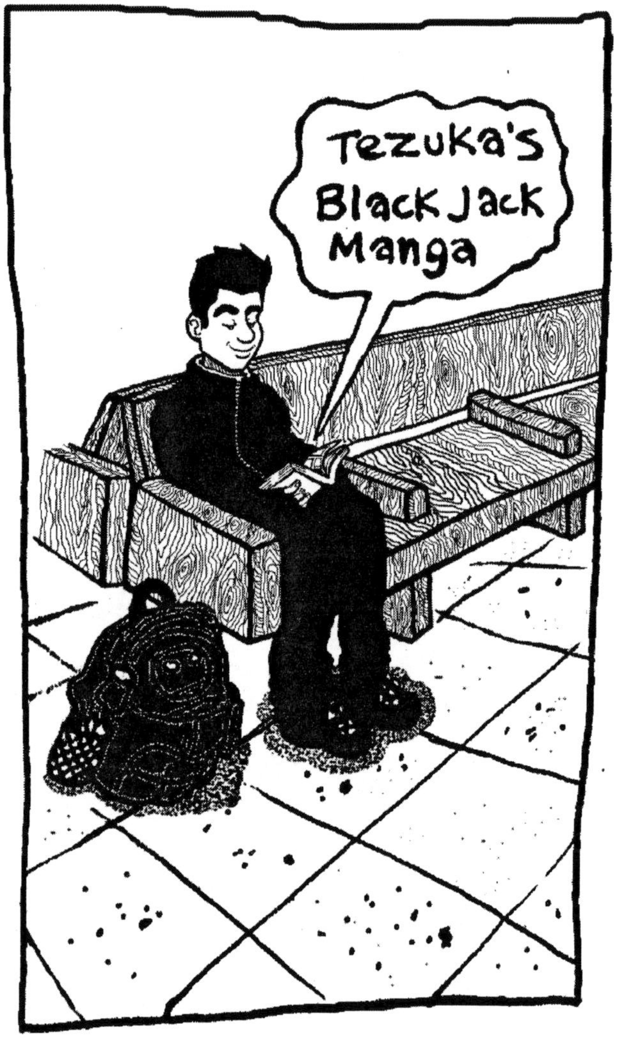
Tezuka's
Black Jack
Manga

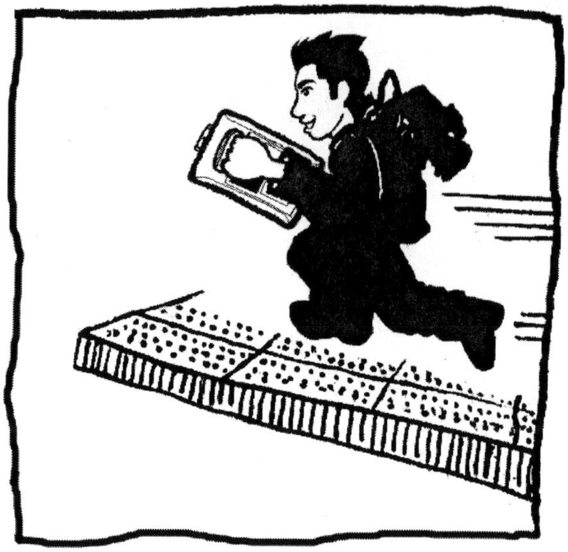

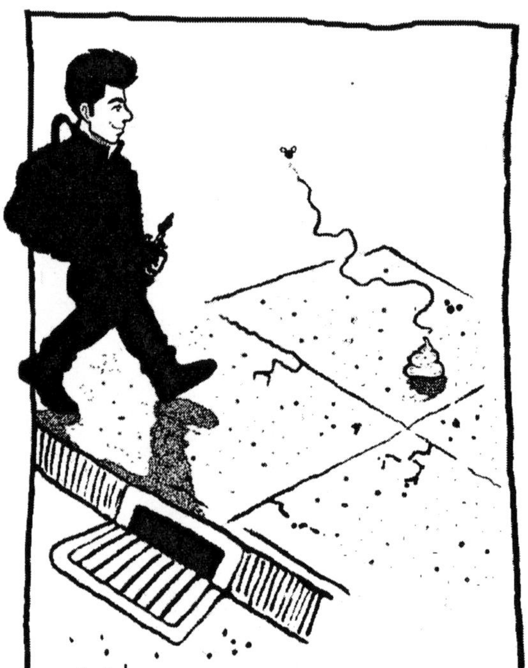

The Subway Sketch Artist

I am a Subway sketch artist
A free imaginative thinker
Captivated by specific interests
Distant from the realm
Of the lay person's understanding

It's difficult to prescribe an explanation
As to why the Subway transit system
Has become the source of my inspiration
Why were Michelangelo's creations
Deeply rooted and inspired
By the ideas of divine salvation?
I firmly believe the source of inspiration
Chooses the artist
Not the other way around

Every employee has his cubicle
Every employer has his office
What does the artist use
To define his workspace?
The simple truth is: the world!
The creative process
Cannot be confined behind plexiglass
It must roam freely
Past the eight by eight
Dimensions of the cubicle
It may transgress at any hour
Day or night
It happens right at that moment
When it all just...clicks!

As a professionally trained artist
At the School of Visual Arts
I speak out on behalf of the artists
We have all learned the fundamentals
Supplementing this core education
With our own personal touch
It is what makes us who we really are
My artistic strengths
Resonate in my manga publications
You may be familiar
With this popular Japanese art form
Or perhaps you are unaware
Of the artistic storytelling it provides
The freedom it allows the artist
To express and write what he truly believes

Freedom!

That is the force that rushes past me
The undrawn parallel
Between manga and the Subway system
It is the feeling I get
When I draw commuters on the L train
It is the feeling I get
When I stare out the window
Watching the world rush by

It's no easy task
To change a fixed perspective
To help others
See the beauty I see in the Subway system
Even still every impulse in my body
Draws upon this goal!

I begin by inspiring children!
I teach at the Nest+m School
On the Lower East Side
Educating them about manga
Showing them how
I have translated my Subway sketches
To fit this artistic form
They are curious, open minded
If even one of them becomes a professional artist
Detailing my class
As the source of his inspiration
My work is truly complete!

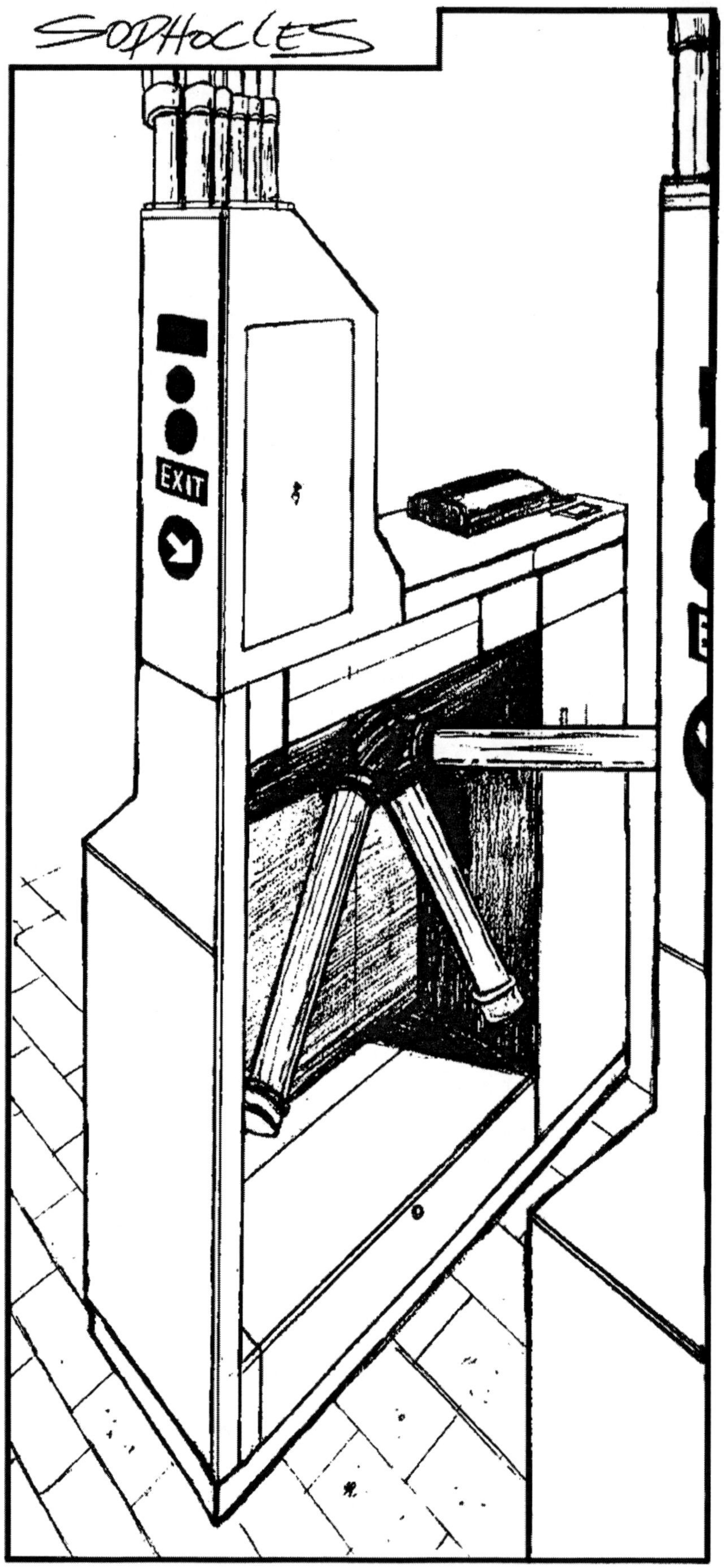
SOPHOCLES
EXIT

The Gatekeeper

So you've decided to travel
Using the Subway?
We just hope you realize
What is expected from you

We don't care if you're young or old
If you're rich or poor
In a rush to head home
Or see us as … just another door
Eventually … you will need to swipe

Before you grow anxious
Realize every door needs a key
To get from point A to point B
We only charge a two fifty fee

Better yet here's a deal
You surely will never forget
Add thirty dollars to Mr. Metro
And for the week you're all set

So Mr. Metro has been purchased
Time to get on your way
Step up to the Gatekeeper
Swipe and have a nice day!

I wish it were always this simple
Buy a metro, swipe and step inside
But when you bend your metro card
Don't expect us to allow you to ride!

What some of you fail to realize
Is we are the underground bouncers
Open our emergency doors
And you'll set off the earsplitting announcers

Even worse yet are those
Who try to skip over undetected
That summons you were just handed
Shows you have just been clearly rejected

Overall we turnstiles will always agree
Our top priority is helping polite commuters
The kind of people who pay their dues
And look down upon Subway polluters

We'll turn our bars as quick as you need
So you can catch up with your friends
Scratch our backs and we'll scratch yours
Everyone always wins in the end

We operate around the city
Around the state, around the nation
Personally my friends and I
Hang out by the S, 4, 5, 6 and 7
Here In Grand Central Station

So now you face the morning rush
Heading on the Metro North
Just remember everything I said
Be patient and every commuter will go forth

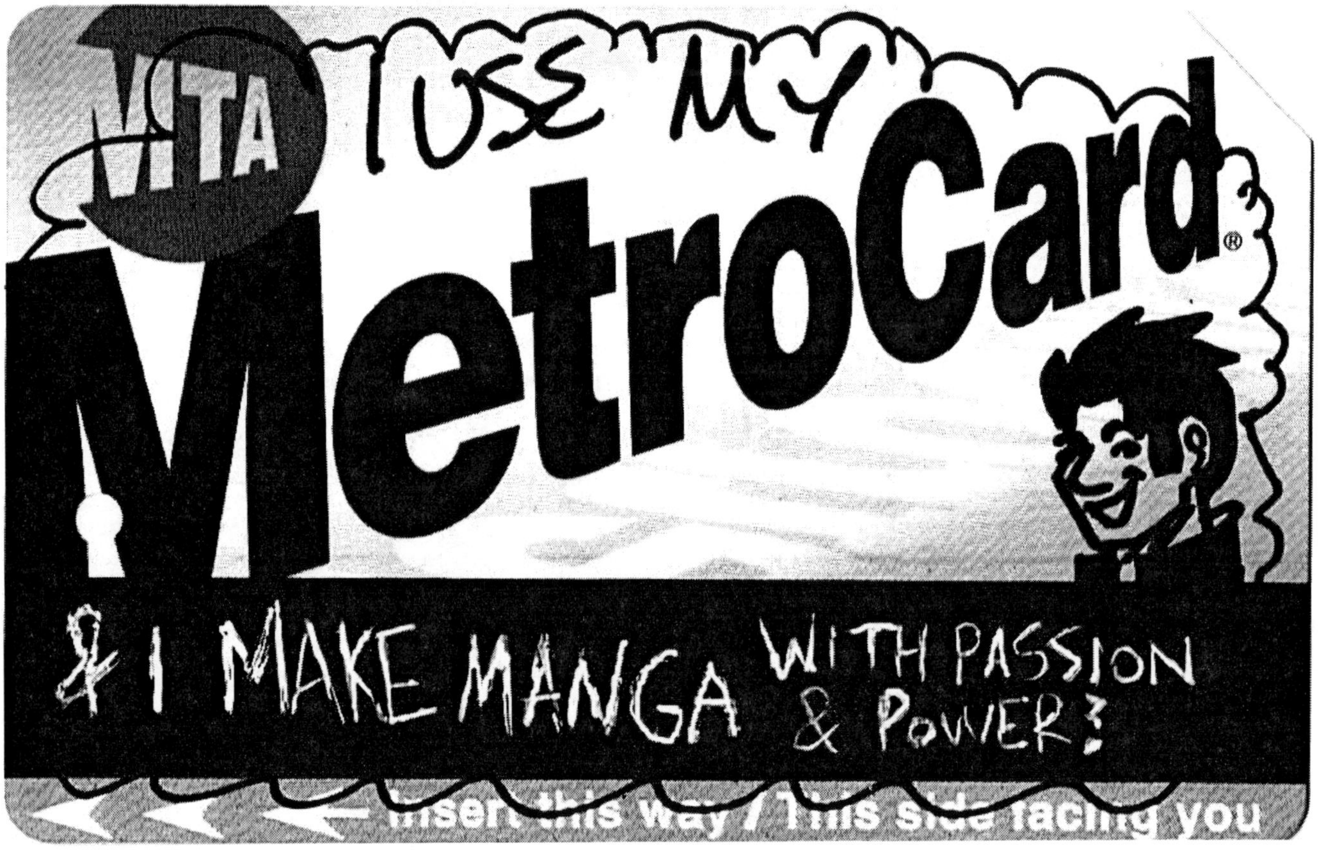
MTA
I USE MY
MetroCard®
& I MAKE MANGA WITH PASSION & POWER!
Insert this way / This side facing you

Mr. Metro

Oh sir, nice to meet you
I see you chose
The weekly-unlimited option

I'm truly excited
What's our schedule like today?
Are we starting downtown?
Going to the museums?
How about we head uptown
For some fine sea-side dining

I don't want to state the obvious
But you are bending me! Ouch!
Let me tell you my friend the Gatekeeper
He's a bit overprotective
So straighten me out
And we can get this train
Out of the station!

By the way
In case you didn't realize, I'm a metro card!
You can call me Mr. Metro

Oh, I see you have another one as well
Damn! Mrs. Metro is looking good
Is that a 2016 expiration date
You are walking around with?
Wow, young and good-looking?
I certainly wouldn't mind
Taking the express train with you
All the way to the last stop
Just playing, but seriously I'm a gentleman
You won't need to call that 511 number
For metro card customer service
Trust me I got your back

Well anyway I got carried away
Hey Gatekeeper!
I got a travel companion with me tonight
Train car for two please

Well it's been a long week
Sheesh I am all swiped out
I mean just look at these stretch marks
Oh my god my bar code is just ruined!

Wait, wait, wait! I take it back!
Don't hand me over to Tommy Trashcan!
No offense but he's kind of trashy

I got a good idea
We work so great together right?
Why not refill me … save a buck
Common it's only fare
Hey, at the end of the week
A dollar earned is a dollar spent ;)

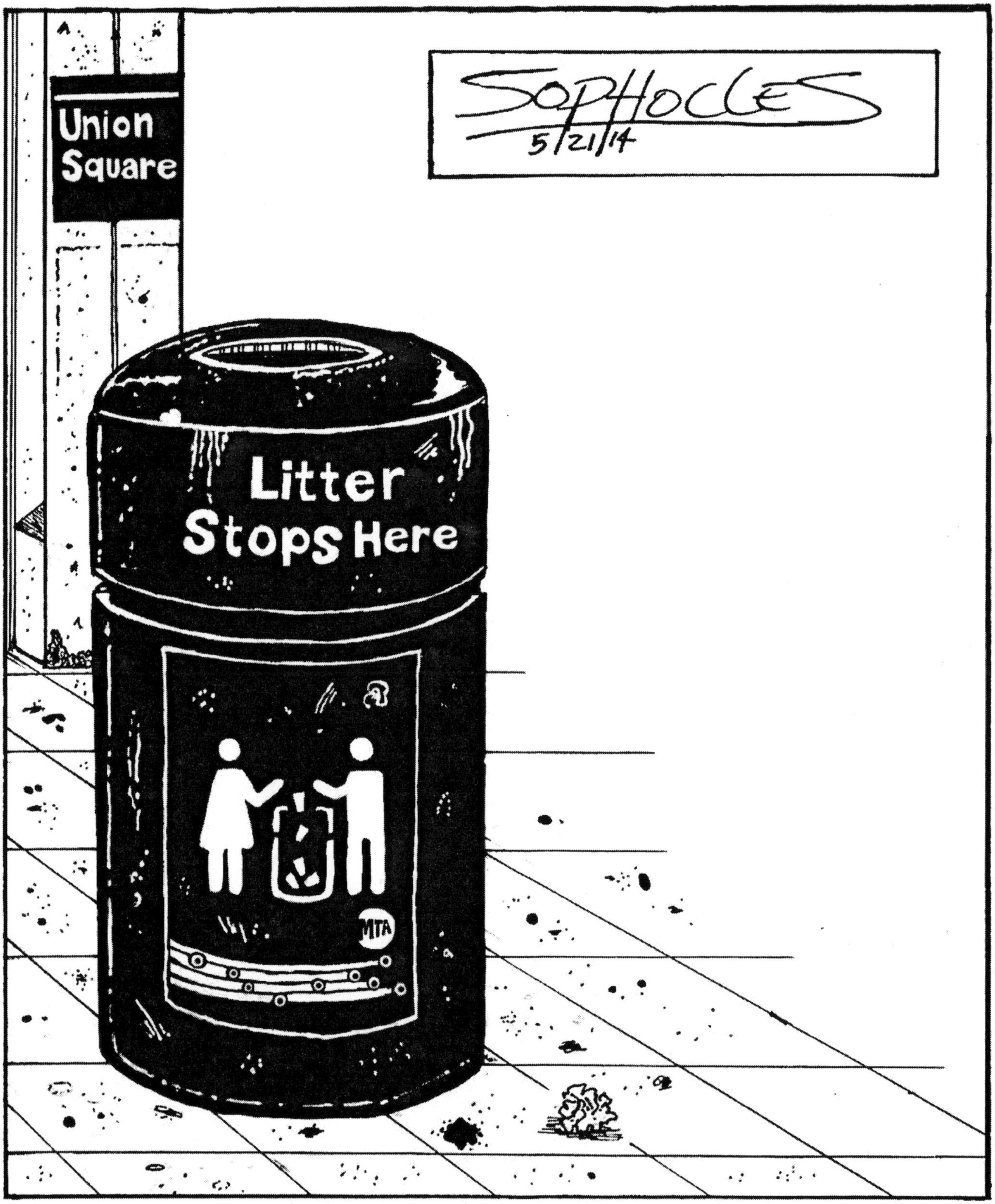
Union Square
Sophocles 5/21/14
Litter Stops Here
MTA

Tommy Trash Can

Another day
My stomach feels full
Excuse me!
Stop feeding me your left over banana peel!
You don't want it and neither do I
Hey Mr. Metro, didn't expect to run into you
Don't they know even when you're all used up
You are still worth something?

I try to speak up whenever I get the chance
But whenever people pass me by
They make sure I keep my lid shut

My name is Tommy Trash Can
What, you don't like it?
Well of course it's a crappy name
I was practically raised by dumpsters, duh!

So a little about me...
Well for as far back as I can remember
I've been placed inside Union Square Station

It's so difficult to find some peace and quiet
Everyone is always yelling
Don't even get me started on the musicians!
I can bang my metal hat
Producing a sound 10 times better
Than what these hooligans are calling "music"

The nights are the worst though...
By day, I at least get to fill up on left overs
Sandwiches, candy bars maybe a Mountain Dew

Nighttime is when the robbers come....
I never see them coming till it's too late
These jerks are so trashy
They steal my leftovers every night
Reaching down into the pit of my stomach
They just clean me out!
Gross!

So today this guy opened me up
Tossed something inside me
It was a shiny box wrapped in ribbon
When I opened it though ... jeez!
It was this ring with a big shiny rock on it!
I've never seen anything like it
I tried to digest it ... but oh boy
This was nothing like an onion ring, yikes!

Another trashcan told me about items like this
He got this cool looking box
With a bunch of buttons you press
All of a sudden! You can talk to someone!!!
He called it a treasure
That's what this must be a treasure

Well tonight those robbers will show up again
Only this time I have something worth protecting
They won't get their hands on my treasure!

Wait that's the guy who gave me the treasure!
He seems really upset
What's he looking for?
Oh wait....
Did he give me the treasure by mistake!
Well shucks I thought he just really liked me
He's looking through the trashcans
Oh wait he's going to look inside me!
I guess he really loves this thing as well

Better give him a tip
Here you go buddy
Bang! Clank!
There you go I'm on all fours
Your box is right there! Pick it up!
Wow well shucks
People don't smile at me like that everyday
I'll hold on to that smile
It's a treasure no robber can take away!

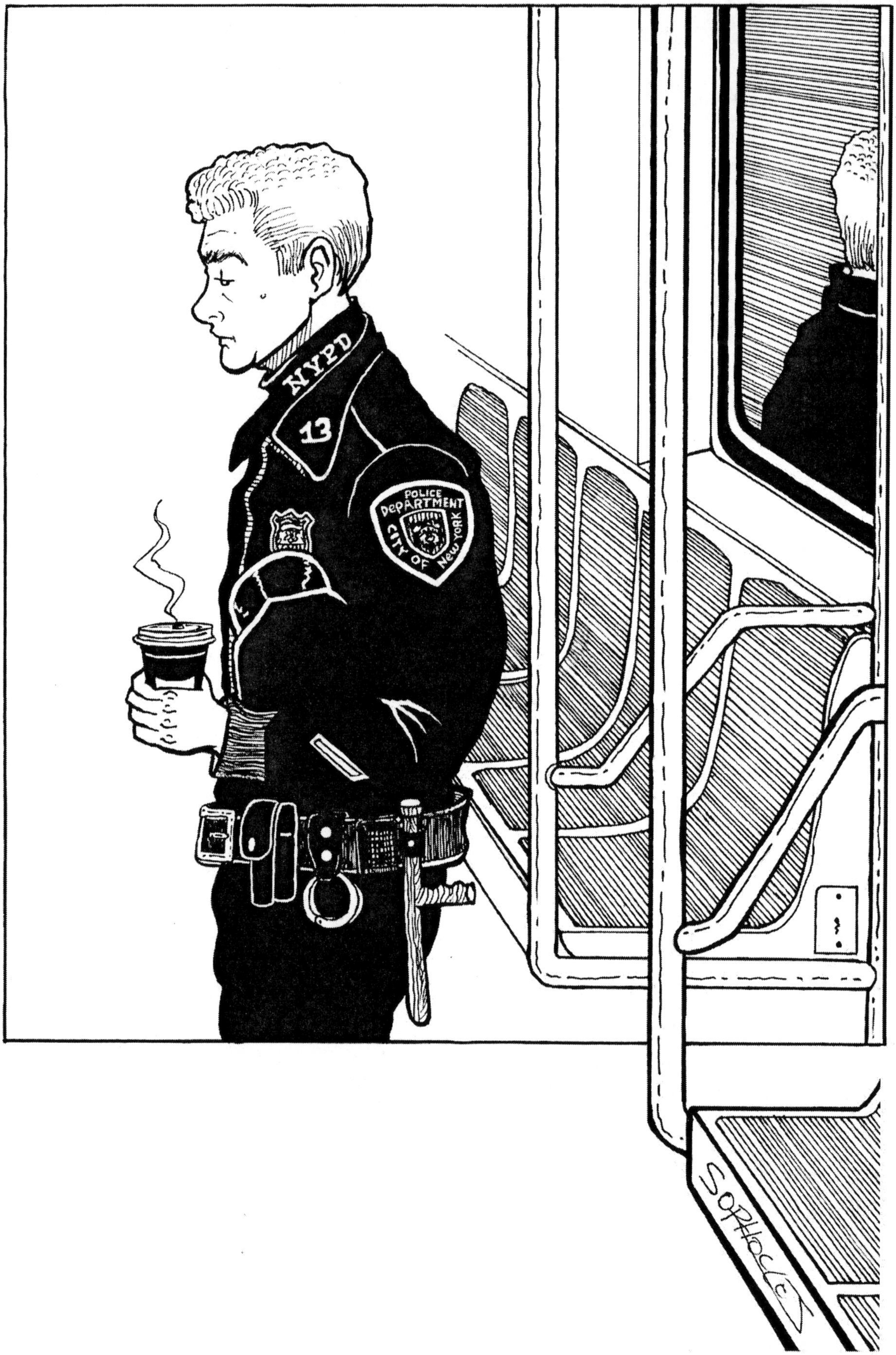
NYPD
13
POLICE
DEPARTMENT
CITY OF NEW YORK

Officer James Connolly

Another late shift, another coffee break
I've been working inside Penn Station
For the past 15 years
Believe me I'm not complaining

Dolled up girls
Getting ready for a night on the town
Free fast food within steps of my post
Oh yeah and probably my favorite part
Plenty of airhead punks
To shove up against the wall
Sorry buddy you are no Jackie Chan
No matter how well
You impersonate the drunken master

Just the other day I had to arrest some guy
For the most ridiculous offense
He was selling stolen monthly metro cards
Right in front of the McDonalds
Here in Penn Station! In my backyard!
Better yet when I approached him
He reached from behind his "station"
With a fresh bag of Big Macs
Does he think I could be bribed so easily?

I have some friends from the academy
They got stuck in rough neighborhoods
Jamaica, Far Rockaway, Elmhurst
I mean talk about a bad break!
They don't even get to take advantage
Of my favorite deal
Free metro card and train tickets
It's all in the shield baby!

Today I've been assigned
To ride and surveil the subway lines
Starting with the 1, 2 and 3 lines
I'll be going back and forth to Times Square
I won't lie, it certainly gets boring
However it's an important job
Also it is a Saturday night
So my eyes are on the look out
For the unthinkable

I was there on September 11th...
Just a typical ordinary day
The first plane crash
Woke me from a deep sleep
I could hear it all the way from Penn Station

I smelled the rising smoke...
Heard the distant screams...
Of those who lost their lives

We lost friends, brothers and badges
It was the first day
I fully embraced what it means
To be a New York City Police Officer

In this perilous time everyone looked to me
For answers, for guidance
I represented their beacon of hope
Like a superhero sent to protect the city

Penn Station is my office
New York City is my home
Every day I stand guard ready to protect it
Even when the shift ends
I seize every opportunity to enjoy
Its cultural events and artistic offerings

Since I'm going to be in Times Square
I think I'll take a few minutes
Hang out near the shuttle
Listen to this new underground band
The Apostles play tonight

It is these kinds of gatherings after all
Which unite this great city
Against all odds.

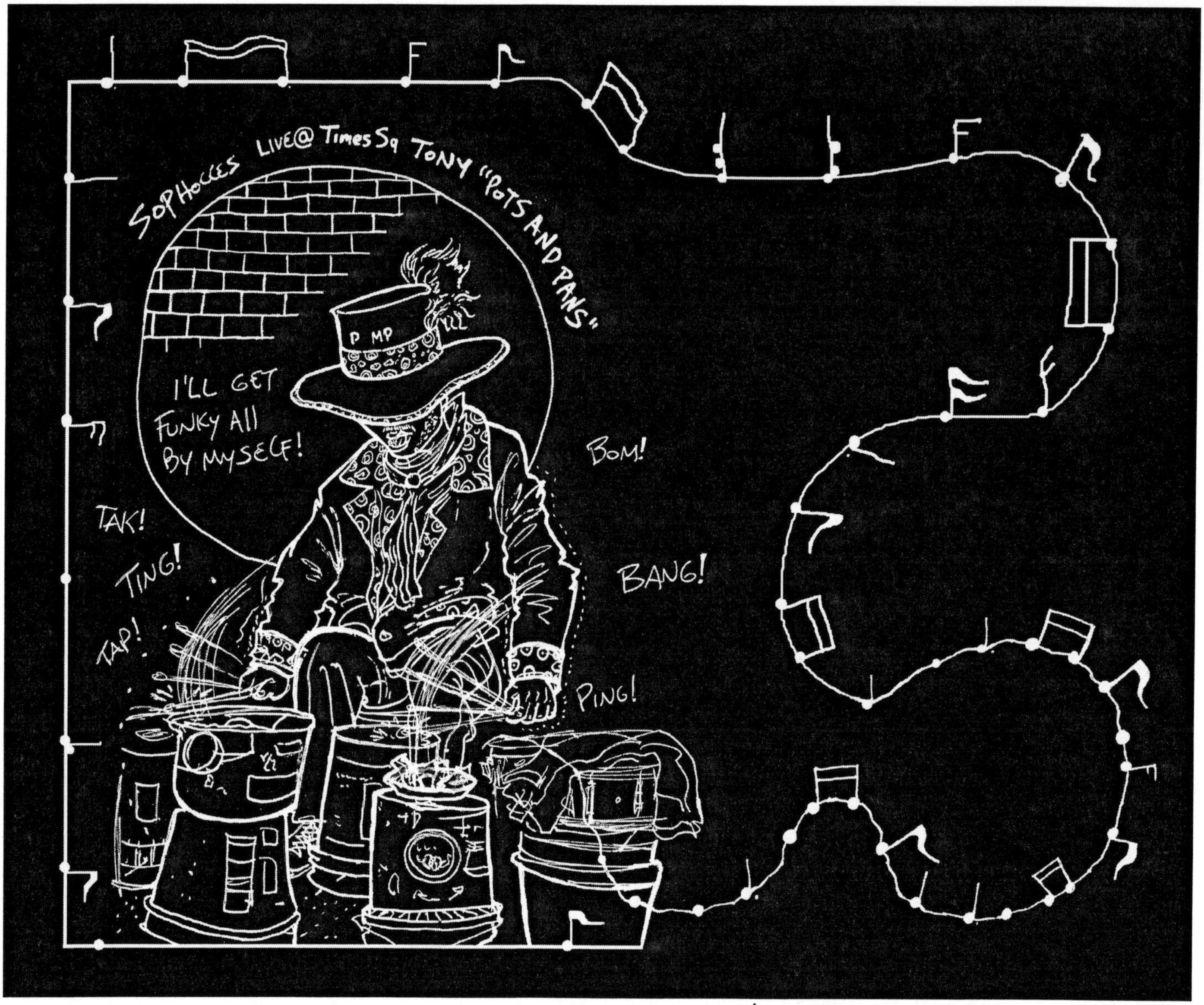
SOPHOCLES LIVE@ Times Sq TONY "POTS AND PANS"
P MP
I'LL GET FUNKY All BY MYSELF!
TAK!
TING!
TAP!
BOM!
BANG!
PING!

Tony Pots and Pans

My name is Tony Pots and Pans!
Come listen to me play
I make real music on these pots and pans
Throw a dollar or two, Hey!
Please put that phone away!

You want to listen and record me on your phone
Watch me play for twenty minutes
And take me home for FREE?!
HELL NO!
This isn't Tony Pots and Pans on demand!
I'm working hard to lift your spirits so please lift mine
Frankly, a donation is just customary

There are some of you who pay your respects
Gladly paying a small fee
Keeping me alive with the strength and will
To share my music with the world
I think sometimes some of you forget
This is how I make my bread and butter
So, let me add rhythm to Times Square station!

The ladies tell me I dress to impress
I am all pimped out
After all, presentation is half the battle
So step right up
Ladies and gentlemen
Just a dollar or two
No need for American Express

Now wait a minute!
Who's this fool stealing my swag?
My fans are swarming near him
Wearing that oversized book bag

Looks like it's a Subway artist
Trying to sell his work
I feel ya brotha, just fighting the good fight

I called him over,
"Hey! Can I take a look?"

He had skills!
I was truly inspired!
When I looked at his work,
I said, straight up,
"DAMN, THAT'S FLY AS HELL!"

This is what we artists do
Whether you are a street performer, musician
Or a Subway artist looking to sell his work
Just remember this…

Every dollar you send our way
Gets paid back ten fold
By what we create
Each and every day!

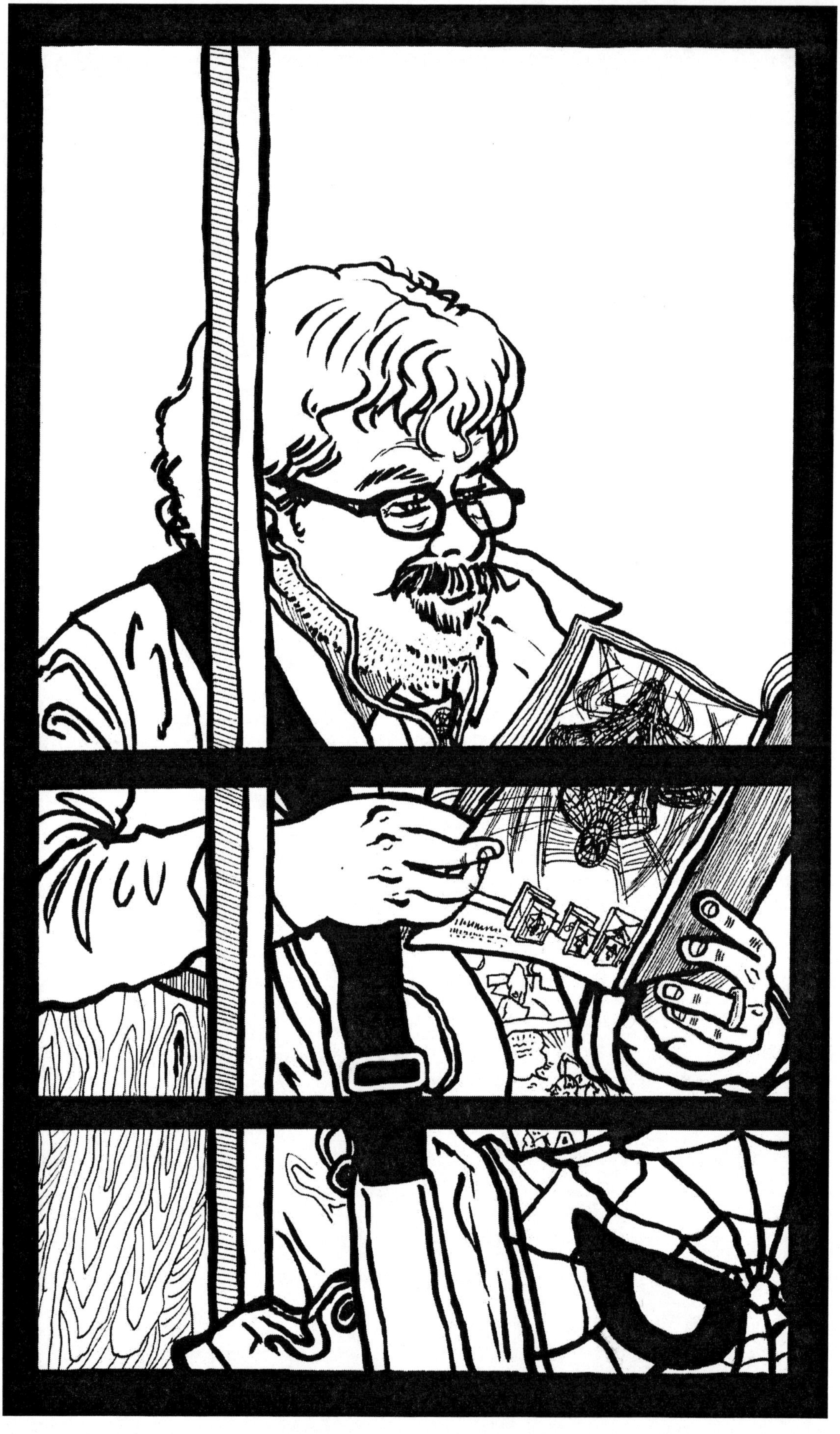

My Neighborhood Spider-Man

Web slinging!
Great power!
Great responsibility!
Peter Parker and the latest villain
That's right
The new Spider-Man movie is playing!
Harry and I have been reading comics
Since Stan Lee and Steve Ditko
Introduced us to Spider-Man

We were ten years old
Two kids buried under a mound
Of comics and fan art in my basement
It was as if…
He was one of our neighborhood friends
Peter Parker
Born and raised in Forest Hills
Like we were
Every issue, every print
Every collectible and action figure
I have them all

Spider-Man was and continues to be my idol
My guiding role model who represents more
Than an action hero or comic book fantasy

Reading through the comics
The images flashed in my head
Like sequential scenes in a film
When the first three films were released
It's as if everything I had imagined
Had been playing in the minds
Of the writers and producers
Like they had taken the liberty of
Broadcasting my vision
On the silver screen

When I thought it could not get any better
Sony Productions rebooted the franchise
Getting off to a strong start
Spider-Man once again grabbed my attention
Introducing himself
To a new generation of adoring fans
Finally now after all these years
The movie I have truly been waiting for
Has made its way to the silver screen

Electro was cast as the villain for this film
In many ways
I find him to be the most relatable villain
Just like Electro…
I sometimes feel underappreciated
By the people I look up to the most

Almost every film
Encourages their audience
To root for the protagonist
What about the antagonist?
What fuels them? Should they not be
Analyzed and appreciated in the same way?
An important and necessary contribution
To a captivating and memorable story

Earlier today I stopped by Midtown Comics
For free comic book day
The long lines and buzzing crowd
Only got me more excited to see the film
Oh and I suppose
Seeing it in IMAX helps a bit too!

So I took the E and B to Lincoln Square
And met up with Harry in front of the theatre
He was just as excited as I was
When we sat down in the theatre
I noticed my hands were trembling
Preview after preview
Flashed across the screen
Building the anticipation
Finally the show begins!

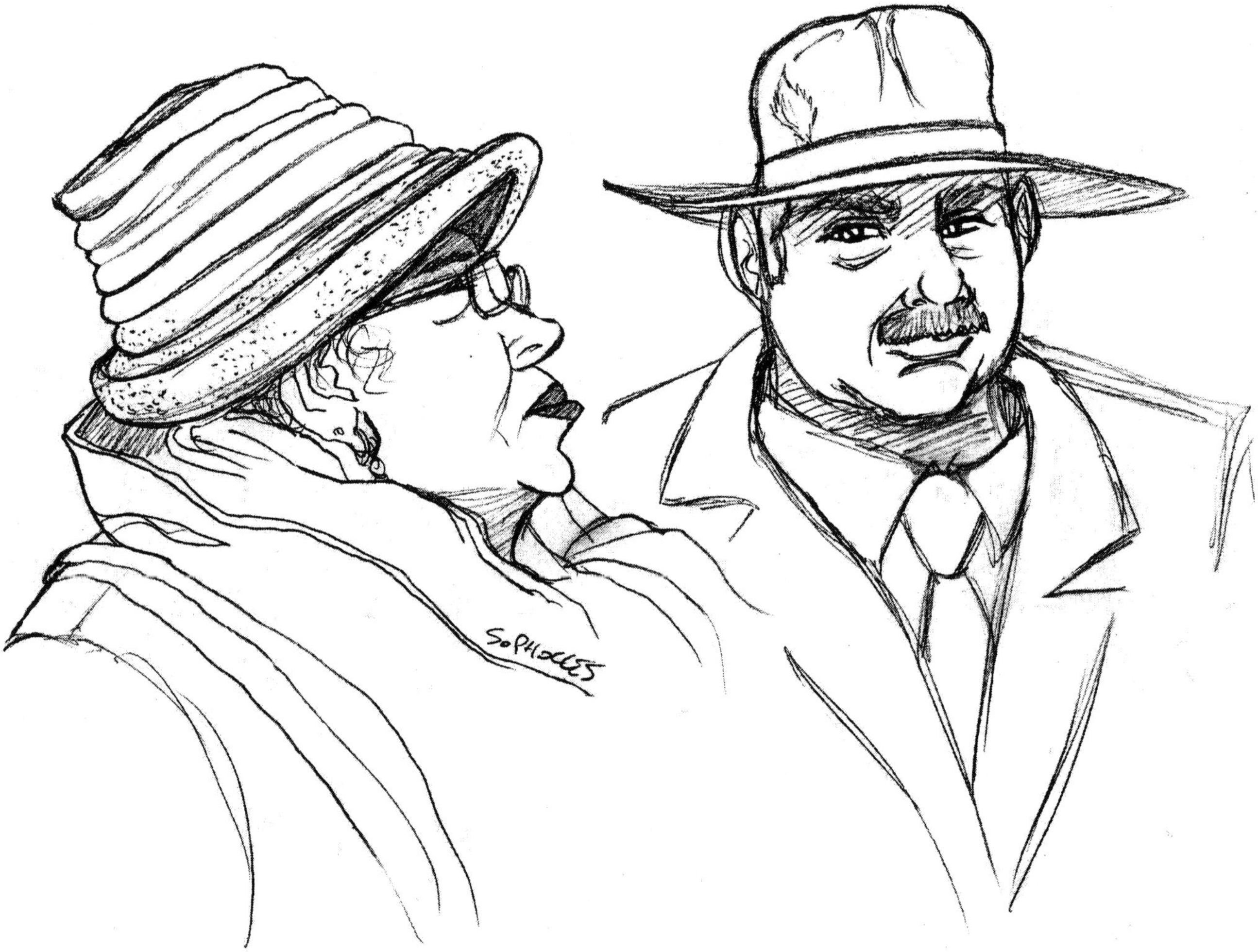
SoPHOCLES

Golden Anniversary

He forgot!
And this time
It wasn't just the toilet seat...

You're kidding me right?
Today is our golden anniversary
50 years of eating and sleeping next to you
There better be an out of this world, good reason
You're not here right now
I'm waiting in Times Square

Ugh knowing him he's probably…
Sleeping on the couch
Watching the game
Playing cards with the neighbors
Watering that damn cactus
He keeps in our bedroom!

Oh God what if…
What if he got lost on the Subway
Got in an accident
Or worse yet … what if he was held up!!!
By one of those "street entrepreneurs" yuck!
Using napkins as business cards!

And yet … it can be any of those
As long as it's not because of her!
Jessica … The gym teacher in apartment 3b
That teenage looking yoga instructing Barbie doll
She had the nerve to knock on my door once!

All of my calls are going straight to voicemail
Maybe if he would show up for our anniversary
I would consider surprising him with an IPhone

On second thought
The way he worships his television
If I got him another shiny screen
He'd probably pay no attention to me

Ugh! Come on Fred!
You're forty five minutes late!
We probably lost our reservation
This whole night is ruined!
Oh he doesn't even know what's coming!
When he shows up I swear
He won't be able to read the paper for a week
We'll see how good Ms. Barbie doll looks like
When I take away his reading glasses
That ought to teach him a lesson!

Well look who finally decided to show up!
Fifty-five minutes a fashionably late entrance
To the most important anniversary of our lives
And yet … even though I'm mad
I'm just glad he's ok
The flowers and chocolate in his hands
Didn't hurt either ;)

At this point I'm absolutely starving!
Sure enough our reservation has disappeared
That's when my husband surprises me
We didn't have a reservation in Times Square
This sly old dog went behind my back
Booking a reservation to my favorite restaurant!!!
Kyklades in Ditmars, Astoria
I can't help but be impressed
On a Friday night it's always packed!

So we take the Q from Herald Square
And during the entire train ride
He holds my hand
With his other, he gently strokes my hair
He tells me he loves me
And all of my fears just melt away

Sometimes it takes a rough start
To appreciate a smooth finish
Ditmars Boulevard here we come
Here's to a golden 50th anniversary!

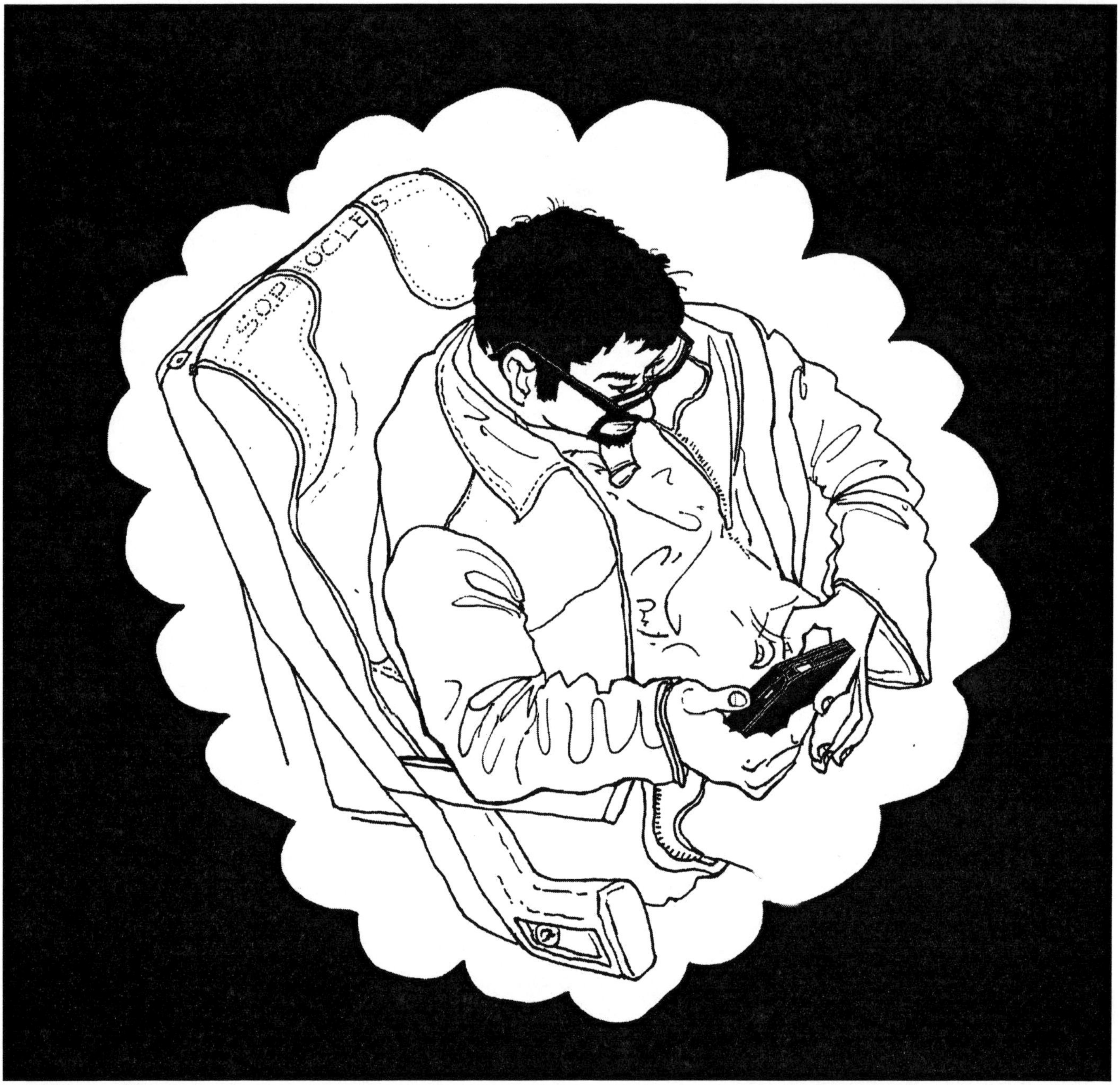
SOP OCLES

Conducting Poetry

"He is 10 minutes late"
"Who are you talking about?"
"Apostolos, the poet do you remember him?"

"Why is he so special Bill?
He is just another commuter
Just another ticket to punch
The 6:30 train to Penn Station am I right?"

"Well, Rich lets be real
Being a train conductor gets pretty boring
One day I asked him what he
Was typing on his cell phone
It was a poem about the Subway
I was intrigued so I asked him
Who knocked upon his chamber door?
He laughed … what can I say poetry humor"

"Ok let's focus on our work for today
We can't all be stringing words together
About flowers and daisies"

"Hah! Rich you may not be a poet but
You're quite the comedian
Oh wait! There he is!
He's looking for an outlet
Probably to type up another poem

I recall him saying
He is working with an artist
On publishing a book
If I am not mistaken
I think it's about the Subway!"

"Seriously Bill … who cares!
Did you check his ticket?
That is all I care about!
Do you want to spend your days
No salary no benefits?
I didn't think so!"

"Alright relax Rich."
"Hey wait!"
Did you see that?
He left his wallet behind!
Hey Mr. Apostolos excuse me!"

"Bill will you keep it down!
We are conductors, not maids
Babysitting these grown men"

"I know … but he is different
His poetry is insightful
It isn't just pretty words
You should be more open minded Rich".

"Oh woopty doo! Let me guess
You became a connoisseur of poetry
After attending my wife's poetry club
You know if you don't start punching tickets
You'll be working at Hallmark in no time!"

"Look Rich I'm just saying
Didn't you ever dream of being
Something besides be a train conductor?
Sometimes I feel inspired to write things
Seriously there is no need to
Make fun of him
He looks much happier than us anyway"

"Alright be quiet already sheesh
I need to make the announcement
This is the train to Penn Station
The next stop is … Penn Station"

"Ok Rich, I am just saying
You could learn a thing or two
From a guy like Apostolos
Sometimes the ones who talk the least
Have the most to say.

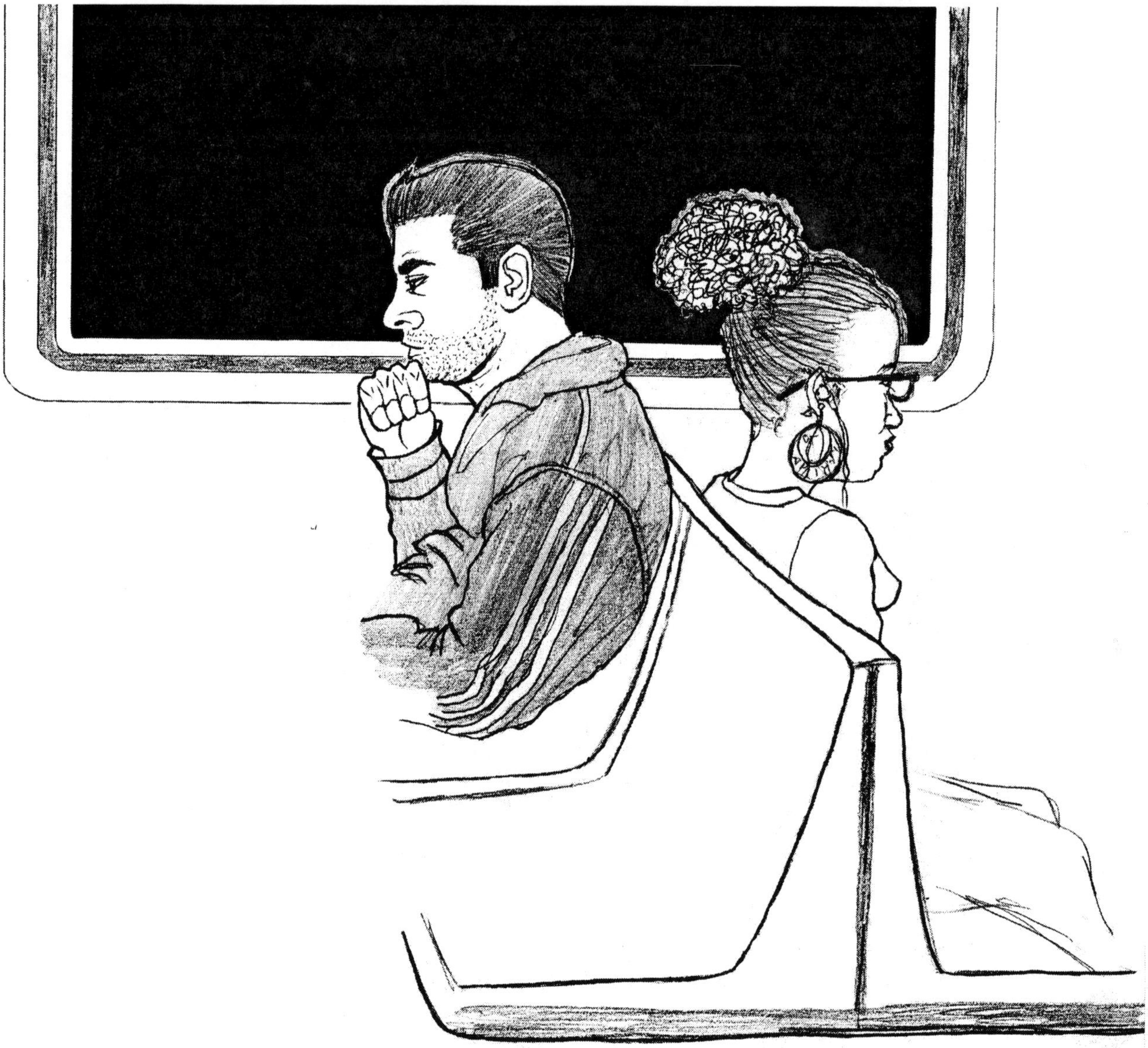

Romantic Railway

Strawberry blonde hair
Glistening under the sun's reflection
Rosy red lips
Delicious and mouth watering
I try not to stare but I can't help myself
She wears her smile like a crown
Magnetizing beauty
A radiant goddess

There's so many thing I want to say
Things I wish to tell her about
I'm stuck
I've written the whole essay
Of our lives together
But I can't figure out the title
Or the opening sentence
"Nice weather we are having?"
Simply too generic
"How are you?"
I bet she gets that all the time

She can walk away any second
Even still I just keep waiting
As if I need
To catch her at the very last second
Stop staring at your watch!
Trust me, It does not have the ability
To help you out with this
Ok seriously though
I should just bump into her and say hello.

Hmm who is that guy?
Why does he keep staring at me?
Is he staring at his watch?
Thinking I won't notice him staring at me
He is kind of cute, in a creepy way I guess
Why doesn't he just come over here?
Just bump into me and say hello, sheesh!
Hmm who knows maybe I am wrong

Well my stop is coming up
We're almost at Times Square
Now is your chance Romeo
Just ask, what's the big deal?"

"Hello, my name is James
I just wanted to say, um
You caught my eye. I mean that
You look beautiful and I
Think that's great! I mean that I
Would like to thank you for
Brightening my day"

"Aw that's so sweet of you
Thank you
My name is Jessica
Nice to meet you"

"Yeah nice to meet you
So anyway I just moved to New York City
I was about to go grab a bite to eat
And if you're walking the same way as me
If you're hungry, I mean well
Maybe if you want…
I mean would you like to ... uh
Would you like to have dinner with me?"

"Sure why not?
Ha ha James you don't have to be so nervous
I would love to!
I'll show you around a bit
We can take the C to Central Park
I know a great place nearby that area"
Oh and James, staring at the watch
So I wouldn't think you were staring at me
Really smooth buddy, here is a tip
Just smile at the girl
If she smiles back, go talk to her!"

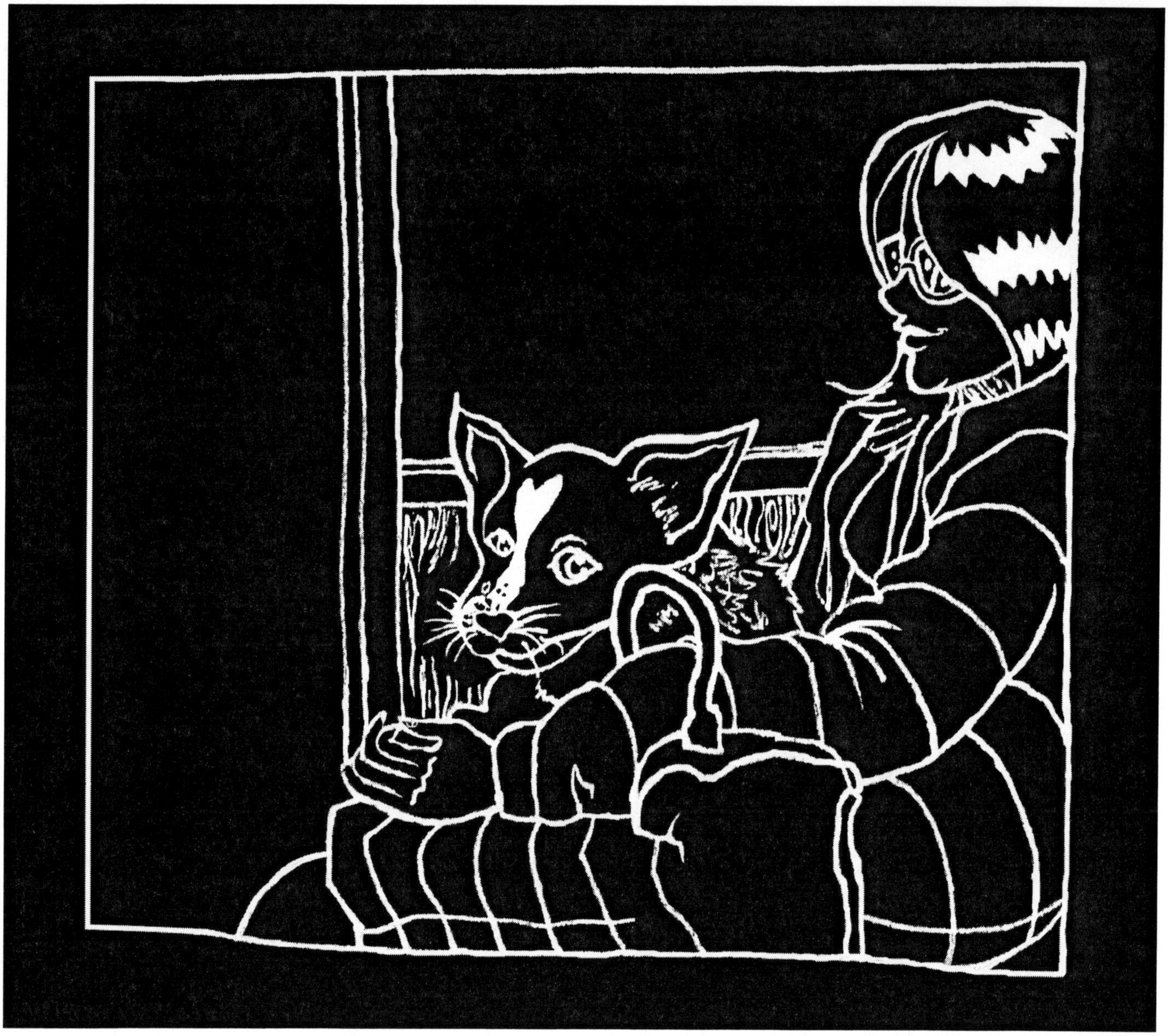

A Ruff Day In New York

My friend is
In the mood
To play catch

Which she normally ruffuses to do
Since her main hobby
Is slouching
In front of the TV
And binge eating
How … pawthetic

This time is different though…
She is ready to go
Can it actually be?
Are we going to
Madison Square Park?
All my friends go there!

We compete once a year
In the dog Olympics
I always get
The most treats when racing

The faster I run to the ball
The faster I get the treats
My friends always say,
"Rufus, you are cheating!"
Clearly they just aren't as hungry as I am!

Were outside of
Times Square station
I always get scared
When we head down to the N train
It barks even louder than I do!

My friend
Loves staring
At the Flatiron Building
But to me it just looks like
A big shiny dog treat!

I am so excited
To walk in Madison Square Park
This winter we didn't really play catch
Which meant less treats for me...
Uh oh!

Wait (ruff ruff) we just passed the park!
Where is she leading me?
No this can't be!
I remember coming here before
NOOO not this place!
(Ruff Ruff) !!!!!!
Not The Vet!!!!!!!!!

Ugh he smells worse than i do!
And that breath, YUCK!
I lick my behind and mine smells better
Oh God, the white gloves!
That means it's needle time!!
Ouch, that hurts!!!

Oh so you are gonna use a weapon on me?
Two can play that game!
Where should i pee on him?
Ah wait here it comes
Psssssssssssssssssssss….
Sweet revenge!

YELP!
He finishes
And doesn't even give me a treat
It's been a ruff ruff day in new york...

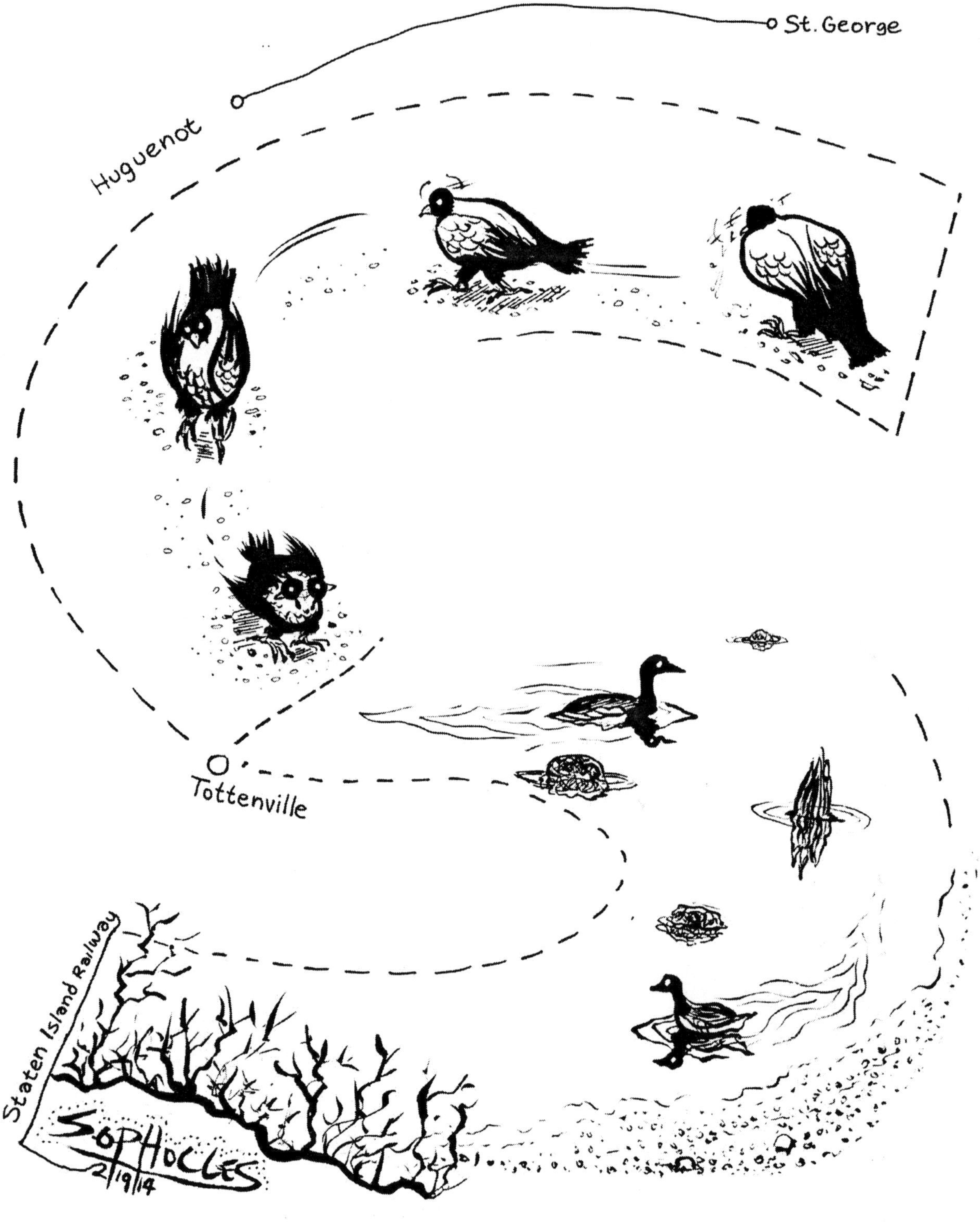
St. George
Huguenot
Tottenville
Staten Island Railway
SOPHOCLES
2/19/14

Wing It

Hey there! Don't mind me
I'm just flying in no particular direction
Actually wait scratch that
Where's the food?
That's where I am headed

Most of my friends
Like to hang out in the park
We have a golden rule amongst us pigeons
Target the children and the old people!
Poop on everyone in between!

Usually I would join them but today I'm headed
To the Staten Island Railway
I've never been there before
I've heard about these big shiny birds
They fly by every 30-45 minutes
I really want to see them!
Maybe they'll teach me how to fly like that!

I've heard it is....
Larger than a fully grown hawk..
Louder than the screech
Of a beach side seagull!
More powerful than a bald eagle!
Rumor says that it has several mouths
Which open and close on command
I have even heard
It has the ability to eat people!

Oh boy! Where am I?
I got so lost in my own thoughts
I hope I'm headed in the right direction
Whoops! Sorry I just tooted!
Oh God, it landed on that poor girl's head
Well hopefully she's not headed to the rails
Would hate to run into her!

Hmm I think I'm lost
Better stop and ask for directions
"Hey Mr. Rat ... yeah you over there!
I'm trying to get to the Staten Island Railway
Will you give a bird a wing?
Help me out over here?"

"I'm headed to Ratafella Station
You should come with me
It's way nicer than that metal railway"

"I'm going to see the big metal bird
I've heard so much about it
I want to learn how it flies so fast!"

"Alright well fly down south
Till you see the large ferry docks
Fly across the water and you'll see it
I hope you're ready for a long flight
I knew this flappy bird that tried to go there
He just disappeared no one saw him again"

"Alright thank you my bottom feeding friend"
So here I go I don't care what it takes
I'll flap my wings until I reach my goal!

Oh boy! Three hours of flying I am pooped!
There it is! I found it!
The Staten Island Railway!
I'll just flap around here till it comes by
Oh boy I'm so nervous I hope it likes me

Wow the inside of it is absolutely flaptastic!
I'm so glad I stuck to my goal
It was a long flight
I didn't know where I was going
But hey, sometimes if you just wing it
Everything works out!

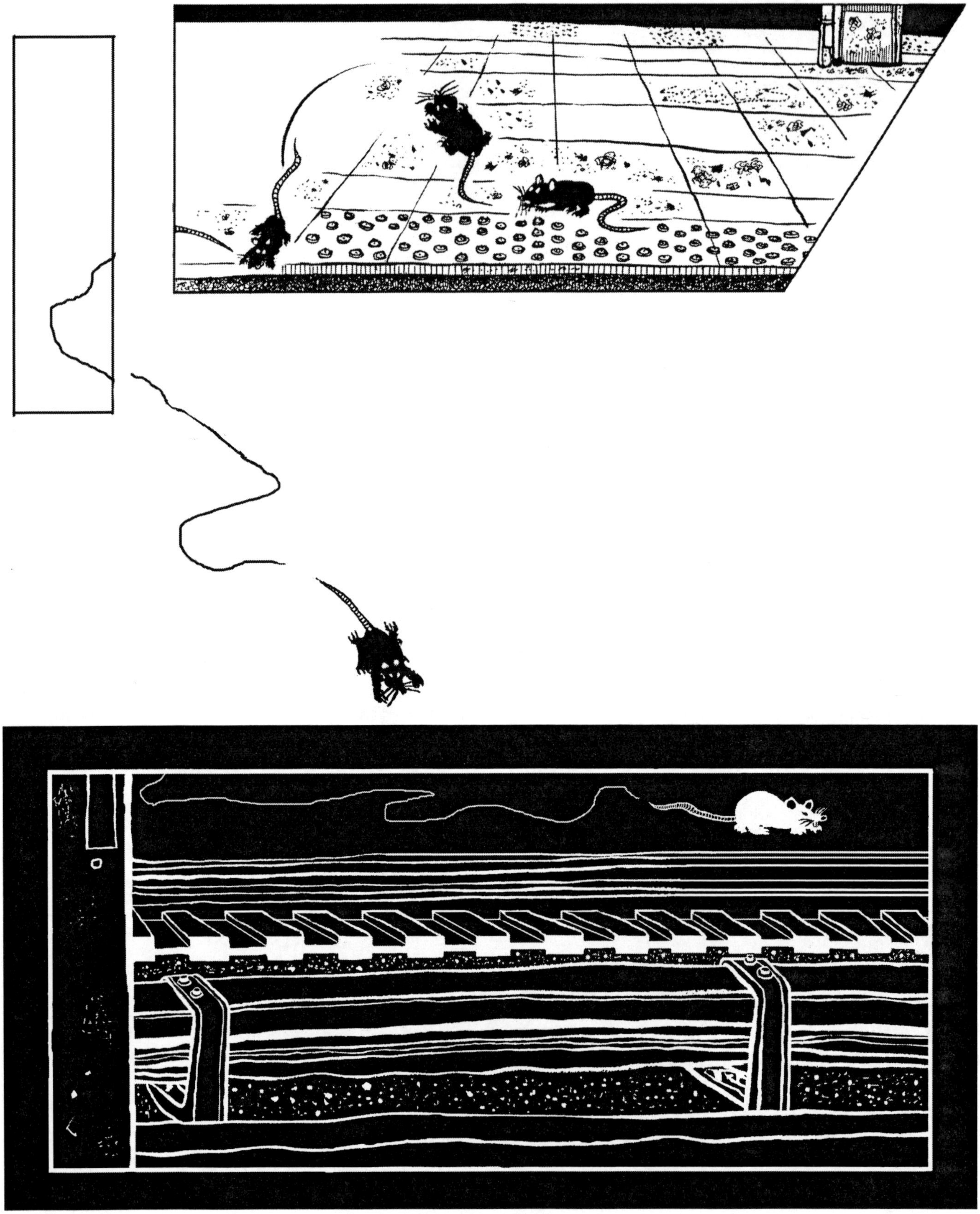

Ratafella Station

Hey Bigfoot!!!
Seriously though
Are you actually going to pick up
That sandwich you just dropped?
Why are you so scared?
Never seen a rat before?

We actually make a good team
You and I
I'm like your personal vacuum cleaner
Batteries not included

We should talk
Seriously … let's grab a bite
I promise I'm a cheap date
I'll finish what ever you leave behind

Try not to scream
It's just me
We're neighbors
Well sort of…
I live in your trash
Whenever you move those bags around
I catch a glimpse of you

Wait! Where are you headed to?
I'm talking to you!
Oh, you're ignoring me?
Well that's not very mice of you!

Any way
My food-tossing friend
We're not all bad
I mean did you catch me in that Pixar film?
We actually taught you guys how to cook!

So this is where you're headed?
Rockefeller Station?
More like Ratafella Station!
My buddies hang out here all the time
See?
We even have the same hangout joints!

Greetings my fellow rats
What's on the menu in this dump?
Half eaten banana … next!
Kale…
Jeez what do I look like Richard Simmons?

You can send that
Straight over to Tommy Trashcan
He has no standards … am I right folks?

Ah wait! Is that a Big Mac with fries?
Well hello there! That's 100 percent beef!
Now we're talking guys!

"Ah jeez something smells down here
Did you cut the cheese or something?"

"Hey! No pushing!
That was my dinner!"

"Oh yeah?
That's your tail in my mouth!"

"Beat it!
Or you're next on the menu!"

"Ah, there's my dinner!"

Good old' Ratafella Station
Da da da dum I'm loving it!

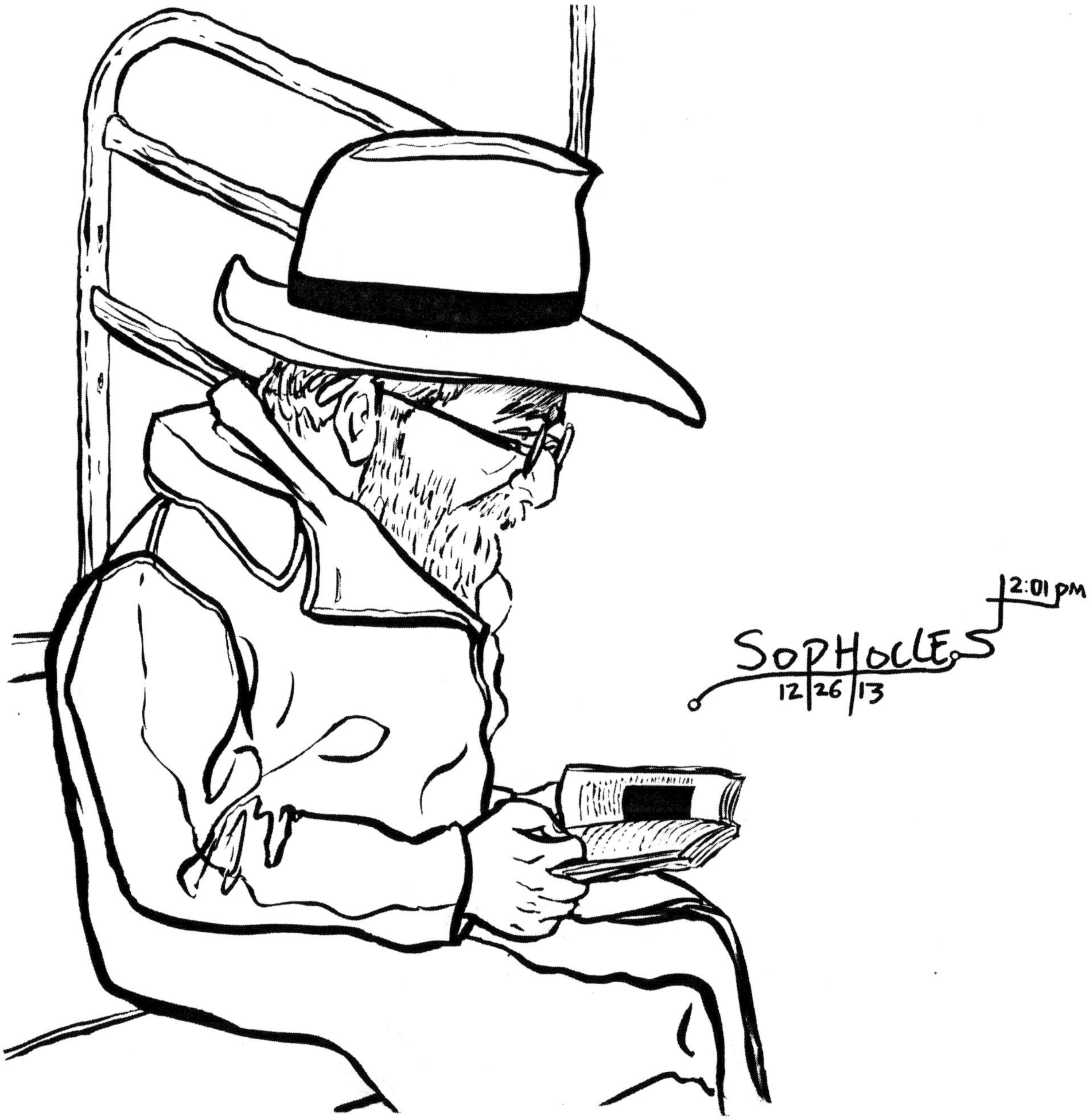

SOPHOCLES
12 26 13
2:01 pm

Elder The Book

There was a time...
You poured through my pages with sheer excitement
Fiction or non-fiction
You treasured me.
As more than just a summer reading assignment

I remember the days you curled up in your bed
You turned on your night light
Flipping through my pages
To clear the thoughts from your head

We set off on adventures
To some distant location
Solved mysteries together
I offered you the greatest gift of all…
A chance to develop your own interpretation!

As you grew older something changed
A creased book, pages faded
You set me aside
For Amazon's number one rated

A reading display
Just a cheap silver screen
With no pages to turn
No desire left to dream

Your adventures now dictated
By a battery life existence
It seems your thirst for knowledge
Has been satiated
By the path of least resistance

You may argue why carry a book with me?
When I can have 100 saved on my device
Did your mother never teach you?
Quality over quantity?

Perhaps you were too distracted to heed her advice.

You've adopted a new line of thinking
More options now means greater reading
But when your text and games share a screen
How can you expect an adult or a teen
To focus on where the story is leading?

Mr. Kindle you should be ashamed
Facilitating a generation of lazy reading
Sabotaged by mindless stimulation
They've lost the patience they'll be needing

To take advantage of the enhancements
You endlessly boast about in your pitch
"Higher quality level reading"
Naive customers eagerly make the switch

As I ride the F train this morning
I look up to my surprise
My owner's carelessly left me behind
To a new owner about half his size

A curious boy flips through my pages
He sees beyond my outdated looks
Perhaps there's hope for this generation
To respect their elders and
Respect their books.

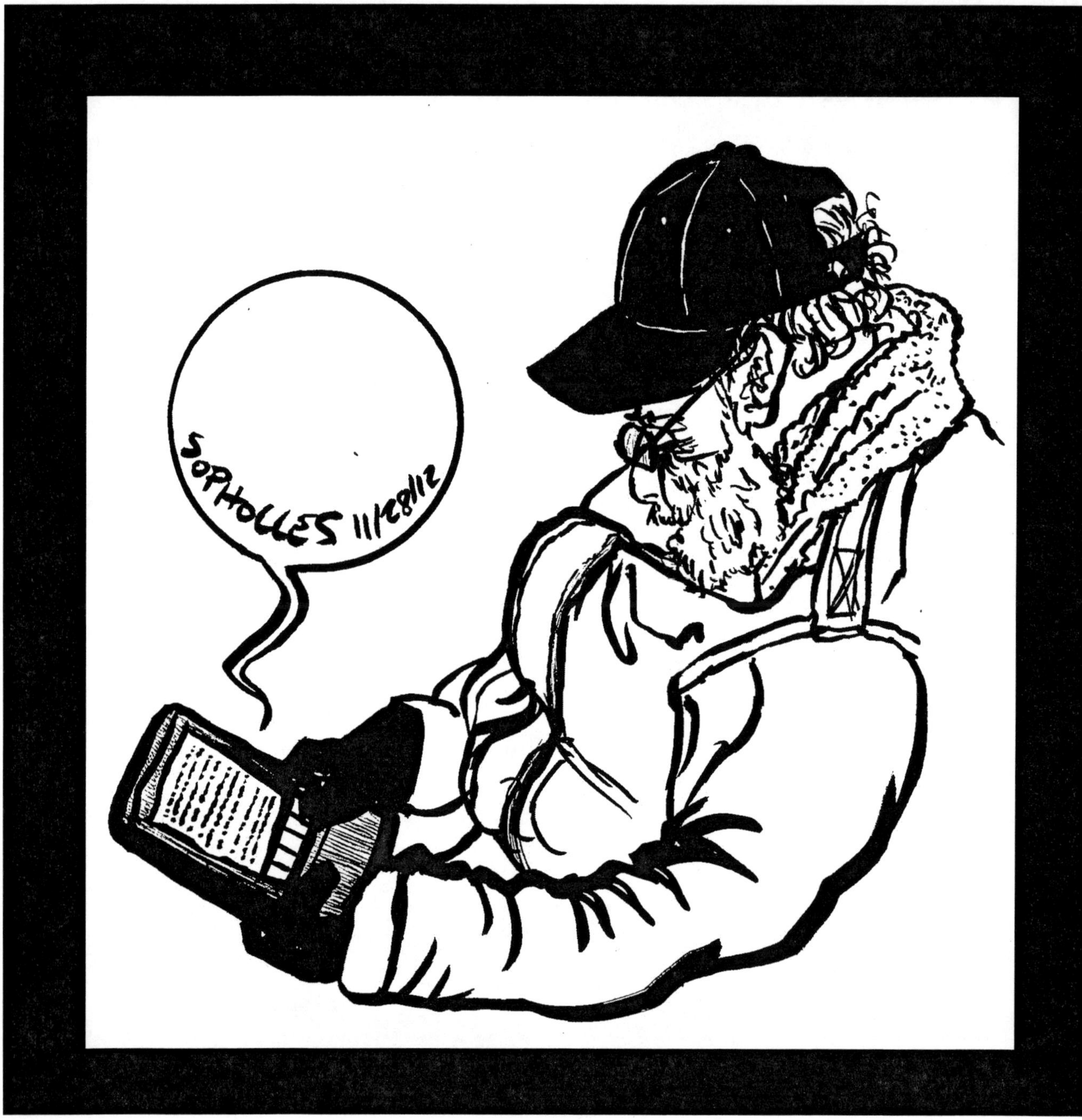
SOPHOCLES 11/28/12

Sir Kindle

Respect my elders?
I provide a zoom up range
Easy reading for geriatrics
You're just too scared to change!

Respect my books?
I pay them so much attention
I provide endless chapter summaries
For maximum retention

Maybe you need to read up
On this so called "battery limitation"
My fire edition offers 11 hours!
Does that meet your expectations?

Have you ever stopped to think?
I'm popular for a reason
I can categorize books and magazines
By the author, date and season

You criticize me for playing a part
In ruining the attention spans of this generation
When you don't even know the functions I offer
Judging me without a moments hesitation!

Now is it because you're feeling lonely?
You're scared of being replaced?
Your significance in man's history
Is being slowly erased!

Are you actually trying to convince readers
My vast library presents a hindrance?
To their ability to independently think
For Gods sakes!
My collection changes their very existence!

I suppose you would cling
To sentimental notions
What are you nuts!
Turn the page, bookmark your place
Well I offer both, with no paper cuts

This guy on the F train
Left you behind and walked away
In Jay St - MetroTech station
I'm transferring to the A

When you finally swallow your pride
I hope you'll come to the conclusion
This snobbish attitude that you're superior
Is based on an insecure delusion!

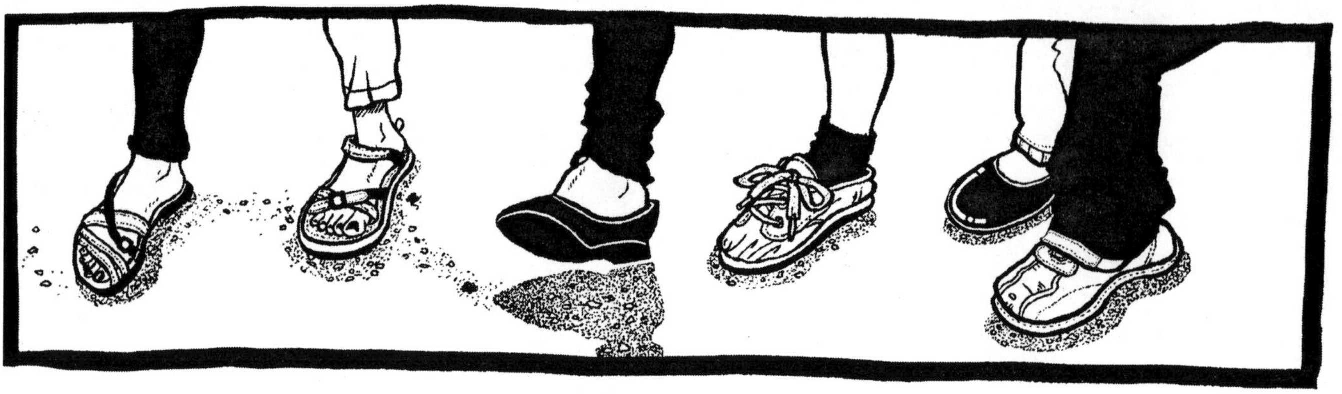

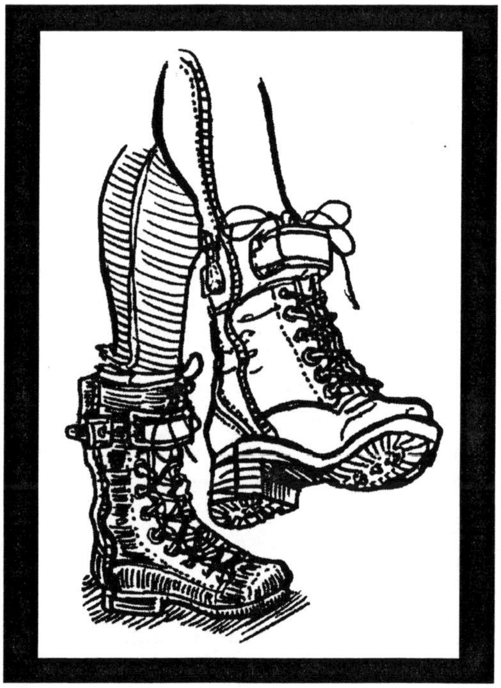

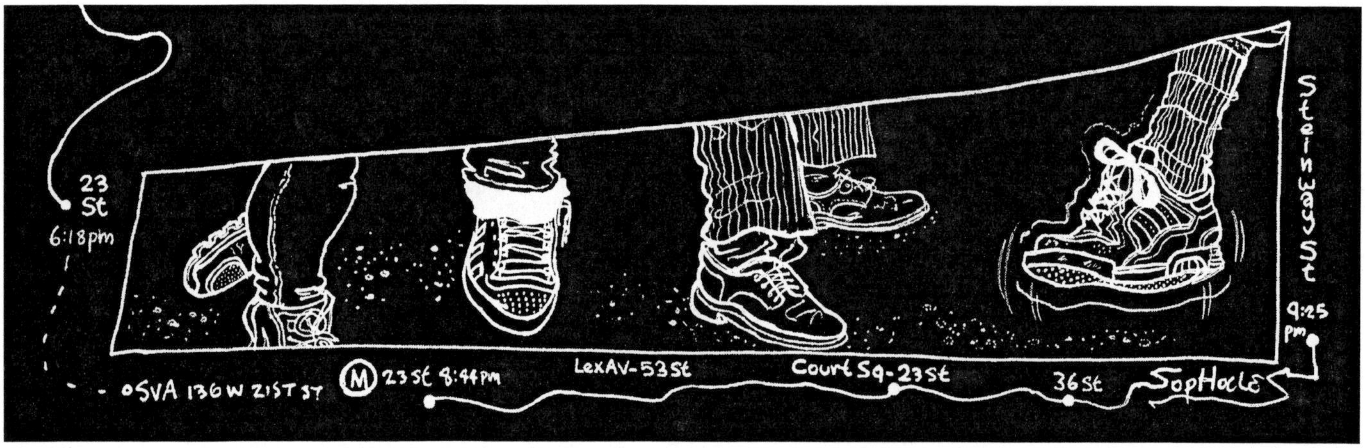
23 St
6:18pm
OSVA 136 W 21ST ST
M 23 St 8:44pm
LexAV-53St
Court Sq-23St
36St
Steinway St
9:25 pm
SopHocLe

Laced Up

All tied up!
Ready to
Start walking

Hey fellow shoes
Nice to see you
At Court Square Station!

What we step on
Is always our top concern

Just another ordinary day
Going to class
Well that's the plan for now at least
My navigator and dear friend
Likes to stop along the way
He is easily distracted by graffiti

Walking down these city streets
I have come across more gum
Than a convenience store
Problem is it was already chewed
I see it caught you too

As we continue our voyage
I bump into some neighborhood friends
Along the way

Did you guys
See Mr. Metro?
Ripped in half
Stepped on, neglected

They hold on to you
Till you're used up
Then when you least expect it
You're rejected!

Remember that bent book
We saw last week on the M train?
Elder would be so disappointed...

My navigator has stopped
It's certainly nice
To take a breath
Our job can be physically draining

We turn away from the university
Are we not going to class?
I strongly disagree
I've walked in your shoes literally
This is where we are supposed to be!

Are you taking me to the shoe store?
You've got to be kidding me
Am I seriously being fired?
I know we sometimes don't see eye to eye
But its not like my soles have expired

Sure enough we're in the shoe section
Wandering Macy's in Herald Square!
I know that it's been awhile
But I thought we were tight
I mean come on…
We've taken so many steps together
This simply is just not fair

So I guess this is it?
Have you made up your mind?
Is this my replacement?
What are you looking to find?
Is the next trip to good will?

The register rings, Ding!
Your new shoes have been purchased
Despite this bitter rejection
Just know it has been my pleasure
To help you lace up

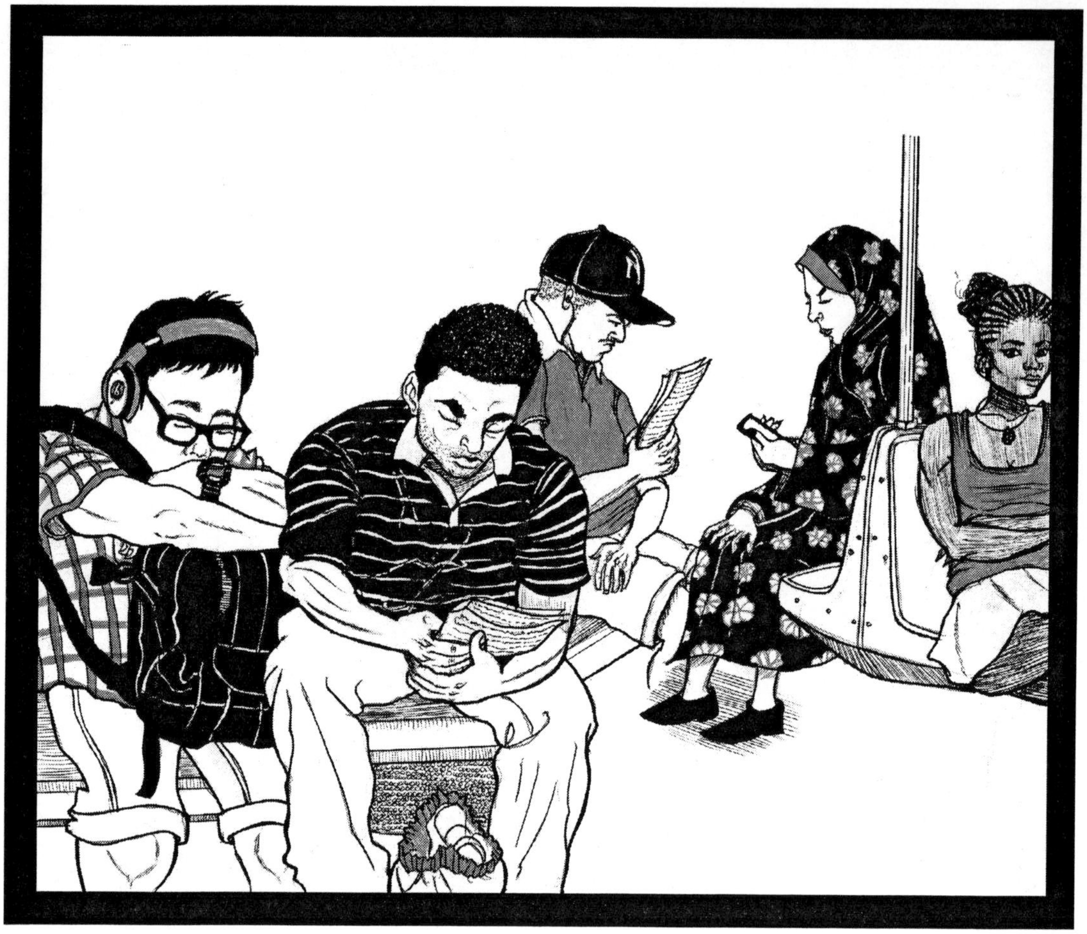

Idle Thoughts

Have you ever wondered
What your fellow commuters are thinking?
Today I am on the R train
I just finished some poems
For my next book.

The young man to my left
Wearing a black and white shirt
Seems interesting I suppose...

The smell of waffle fries and burgers permeate
The name tag and study outline he's holding
Seem to provide clues to his dual identity
You can tell he walks the tight rope everyday
Balancing himself between maintaining
His present while improving his future
Despite his exhaustion, he is content.

Right next to him
a young gentleman
Wearing thick eye glasses
His shoulders have collapsed
As he blankly stares down at the floor
He drowns himself in his music playlist
He is looking for energy, or to be inspired
Those double shifts are never easy.

To my right
Is a young lady
Wearing a red blouse
She stares directly at me
Prying into my own idle thoughts?

A judgmental smirk creases
The corners of her mouth
She crosses her arms in frustration
She seems upset
Not because I'm taking an interest in her
But because no else has.

My attention shifts over to the lady beside her
Dressed in an ethnic garment
She wears her hijab proudly

Her thoughts enclosed within her mobile device
Her eyes dart back and forth
Holding onto every word written on the screen
Her fingers tremble in panic
Perhaps the fate of a loved one is in jeopardy?
As she sits helpless in a moving contraption

But what if I'm wrong?
Maybe she has a husband who is back in Iraq
Fighting as a soldier
She Skypes with him regularly
But on a train with no service
She is limited to an exchange of words
Texting … with no visual confirmation

No reassurance of his safety
Her eyes dart back and forth
Each time she re-reads the words
She can hear a distant echo
Her husband's voice
Bringing her one step closer to him
The train comes to a halt...

At the moment every one snaps out of it
if only I had just a few more moments to observe
Before the doors swing shut

I must press on...
I am heading to Bellmore to see my girlfriend
As I jump on the E
At the Jackson Heights Station
I come across a new group of people
Lost in their own idle thoughts

I am intrigued to say the least...
A man wearing a Yankees hat
Is closely reading through an article
I can see it's about the upcoming Subway Series
His boyish fascination brightens his cheeks
Forsaken dreams of college baseball

Trading in the ball and the bat for the briefcase
Even though he is playing
On a separate but impressive field
I can tell he has a hard time accepting his strikes
And acknowledging his home runs

I have arrived at Jamaica Center.
One more train to Bellmore
I wait for my final ride
I sit back, relax and let my mind drift
I think back to:

The night student

The supermarket worker

The neglected young lady

The distressed Middle Eastern woman

And the unfulfilled former baseball player

Each one has a story to tell
Their chapters are written
In my idle thoughts

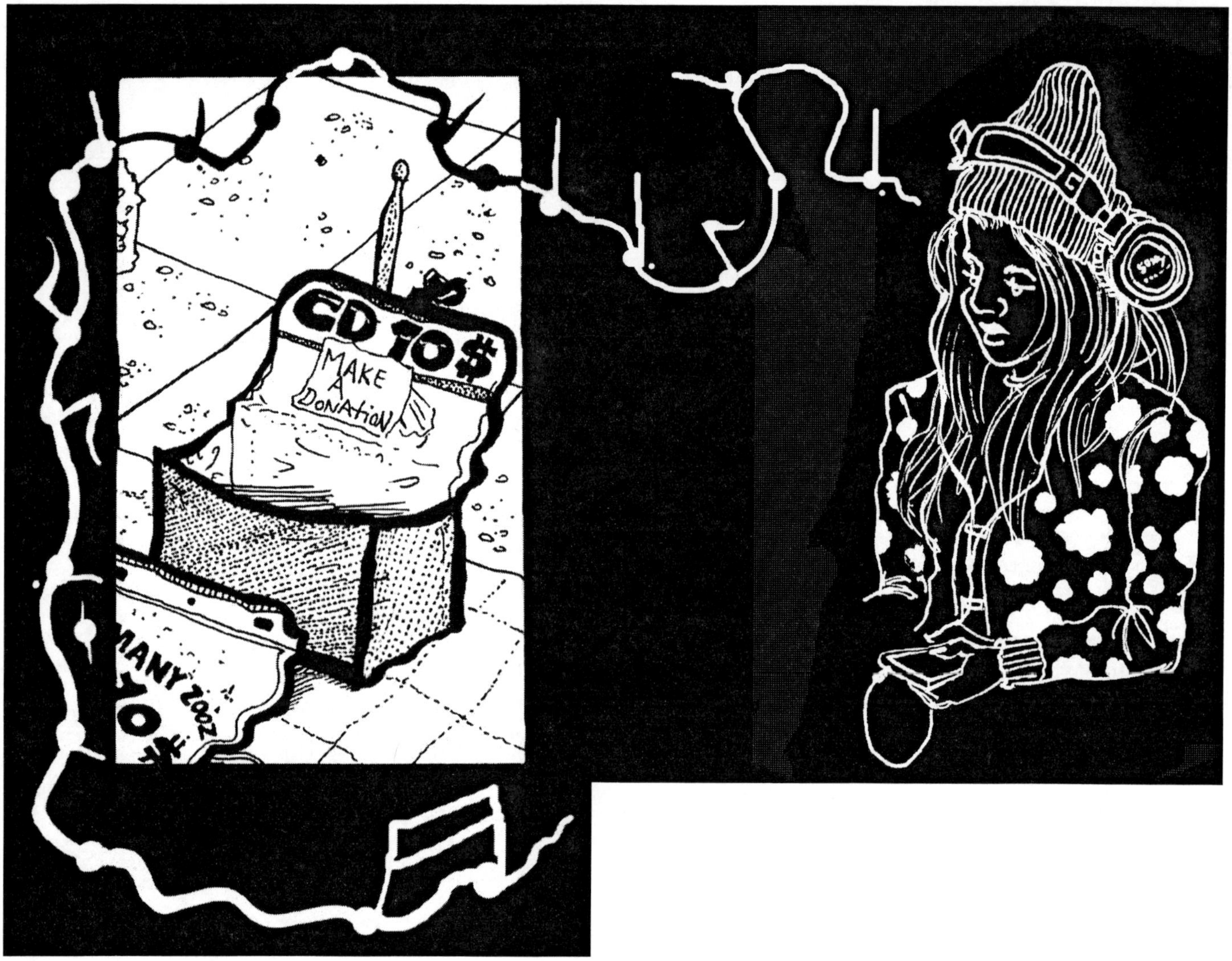
CD 10$
MAKE A DONATION

Music Listening Devices

I remember a time...
Where road trips were passed
By listening to 12 songs
Of whichever CD
Was lying around in my glove compartment

Where pockets were filled
With endless supplies of Double A batteries
Just to hold on to your favorite words
Hybrid theory or The Slim Shady LP
Just a few minutes longer
Before the final drops of juice were drained

Throughout time
Our infatuation has only grown
We've become increasingly reliant
On listening to music
Not just recreationally
But in order to "accomplish certain tasks"

Each device however,
presented it's own set of limitations
In 1877 Thomas Edison
Brought us the record player
In 1982 Japan
Delivered the very first
One album, battery reliant CD Player

As the devices grew smaller
Our musical library grew larger
2001...
124 years after the birth of recorded sound
Apple laid its golden egg

Music listening and sharing was reborn
A device that we continue to rely on in 2014
An electronic filing cabinet
Every artist, every genre
Delivered quite literally
At the touch of our fingertips

Downloading tracks
Replaced buying albums
Sharing playlists replaced purchasing CD's
Everything had changed
Everything had evolved
Everything...
Except for those inconveniences we lost

Those friendly run-ins at Coconuts
Searching for a new album to purchase
The adolescent excitement of a mixed tape
The patience to listen to an entire song...
Rather than just skip to the "good parts"

As the devices have evolved
So have the appliances that go with them
Dr. Dre Beats headphones
Car chargers, home chargers
Anything to make sure
The music never stops

Blaring headphones
Replacing polite conversation
On the morning commute

Near fatal accidents and "close calls"
Replacing city street walking

Workout music and "pump up" beats
Suppressing our own inner voice
The soundtrack of our mind

The evolution of our music listening devices
Will undoubtedly continue
More space, features and stimulation
I'll only suggest, while we look to the future
Faster downloading and consuming
Lets save enough space on our iPods
To store the memories
Of our music listening, past and present.

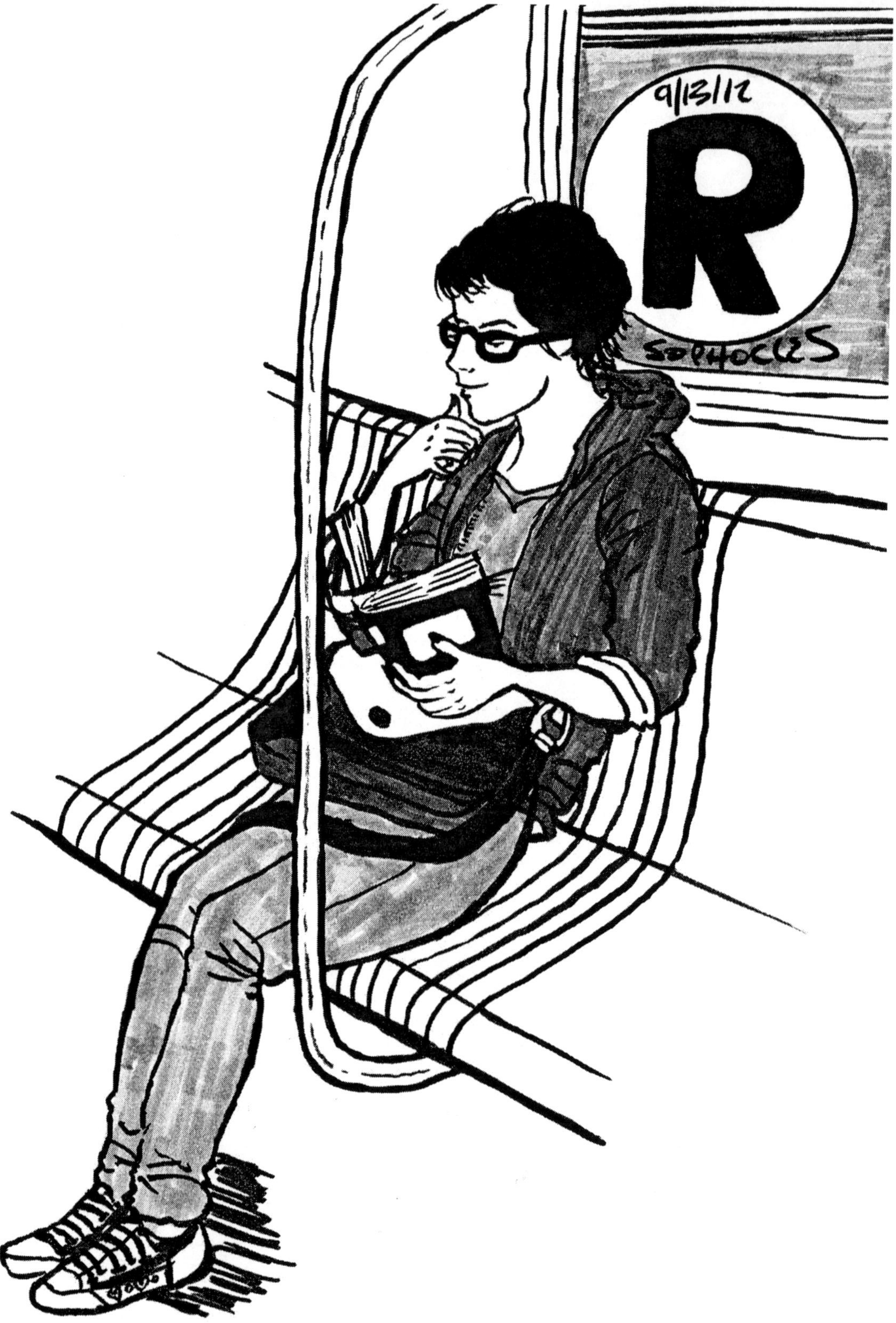
9/13/12
R
SOPHOCLES

Dream Delays

The modern day Greek tragedy
College graduate
24 years old
Despite my best attempts
I am unemployed

I can still hear the roars of excitement...
A beautifully decorated graduation ceremony
Attended by all of my family and friends
When they call my name: Aphrodite Boukas
I remember receiving my diploma
A wave of exhilaration rushed inside of me!

I felt as if all of Patras, Greece
Showed up to congratulate me
The commencement speakers words
"Work today for a brighter tomorrow"
Still throb like a splitting migraine
I cannot seem to alleviate

I've dreamed about traveling to New York
I have friends who have visited
Some whom have moved there
All of them talk about the opportunities
Jobs, career counselors, networking events
Resources I could only dream of!
Patras, Greece was my past and present
Perhaps New York is my future...

Almost as if the heavens were listening
To my speculations about New York
My uncle who lives there currently
Offered for me to come and stay with him
As much as I felt torn
Leaving my family and friends behind
It's called the city of dreams for a reason!

By day I was a PhD candidate in economics
By night I was a curious NYC explorer
Bitter memories in Patras, Greece
Replaced with unforgettable experiences
I shared with friends and family back home

My uncles' New York City restaurant
Went up in flames
With it so did my NYC paradise
After purchasing a new restaurant in Astoria
I figured our lives would go back to normal
They did not...

We fought and argued
He claimed he needed my help
Managing the restaurant, cooking the food
He had lost his partners
I was the only one he claimed he could trust

My studies, my path to become
A high rising international economist
Striving to save the Greek economy
So little girls like me
Can grow up to have a brighter future
Ironically ... gone.

My name is Aphrodite Boukas
I am a dropout PhD economics candidate
A restaurant manager and chef
Most importantly
I am not what I set out to be.

As I step off the R train
Walking down Steinway Street
I will continue to hold my head up high

More than a cook and a restaurant manager
I am a woman with a vision
I will continue to work hard
Be patient and realize my dream
When the right moment presents itself...

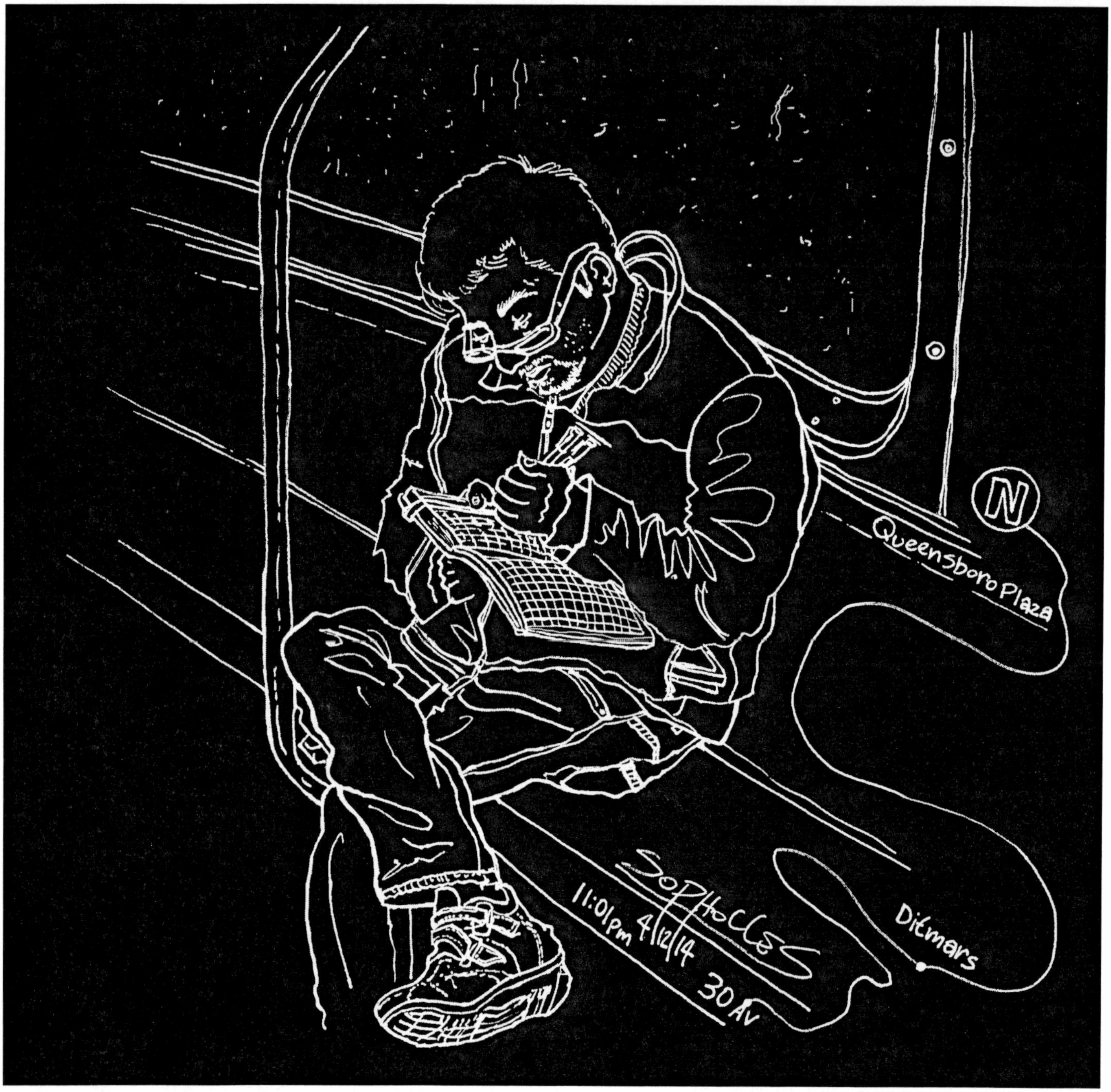
N
Queensboro Plaza
Ditmars
30 Av
11:01pm 4/12/14
Sophocles

Penetrating Emotions

Can you hear us?
Hello?
Do we need to turn up the volume?
These are the penetrating emotions
That swim in the vast ocean
Of my idle mind.
They don't talk much
Since they are always being slightly sedated

There are plenty of thoughts in the sea
When you're fishing around for
Refreshing creativity
The problem is keeping them all in line
As they vigorously try to penetrate their way
To the surface.

Fear.
The immature child within all of us
Even as we get older
This penetrating emotion never ages
It simply diminishes

When we have achieved clarity
When we have made up our minds
The three most important decisions
Who are we? Who do we want to be?
How will we get there?

As we stare
At these intimidating essay topics
We can't help but succumb
To a state of uncontrollable anxiety

Anxiety
She trembles....
In the voice of an anxious woman
Crackling her way to a state of frenzied panic
She needs a minute to select her options.
Deciding whether she will evolve
Into a boiling rage
Or gently simmer into a state of relaxation
After the flame has been extinguished.

Love!
A husband who embraces
An anxious woman
Complimenting her prosecuting objections
With impartial silence and understanding

He waits his turn and when its all over
And she has uttered every complaint
She can possibly think of
He whispers,
"Just know that I'll always be here for you."

Fear, Anxiety and Love.
The elderly gentleman we stumble across
Pouring over volumes of books
Taking notes has experienced them all
In many ways he represents the future

He serves as a visual reminder of
Our constant need for preparation
He doesn't have much to say
He is an optimist
Through better or worse
He has diminished fear
He has silenced anxiety
And has embraced his one true love.

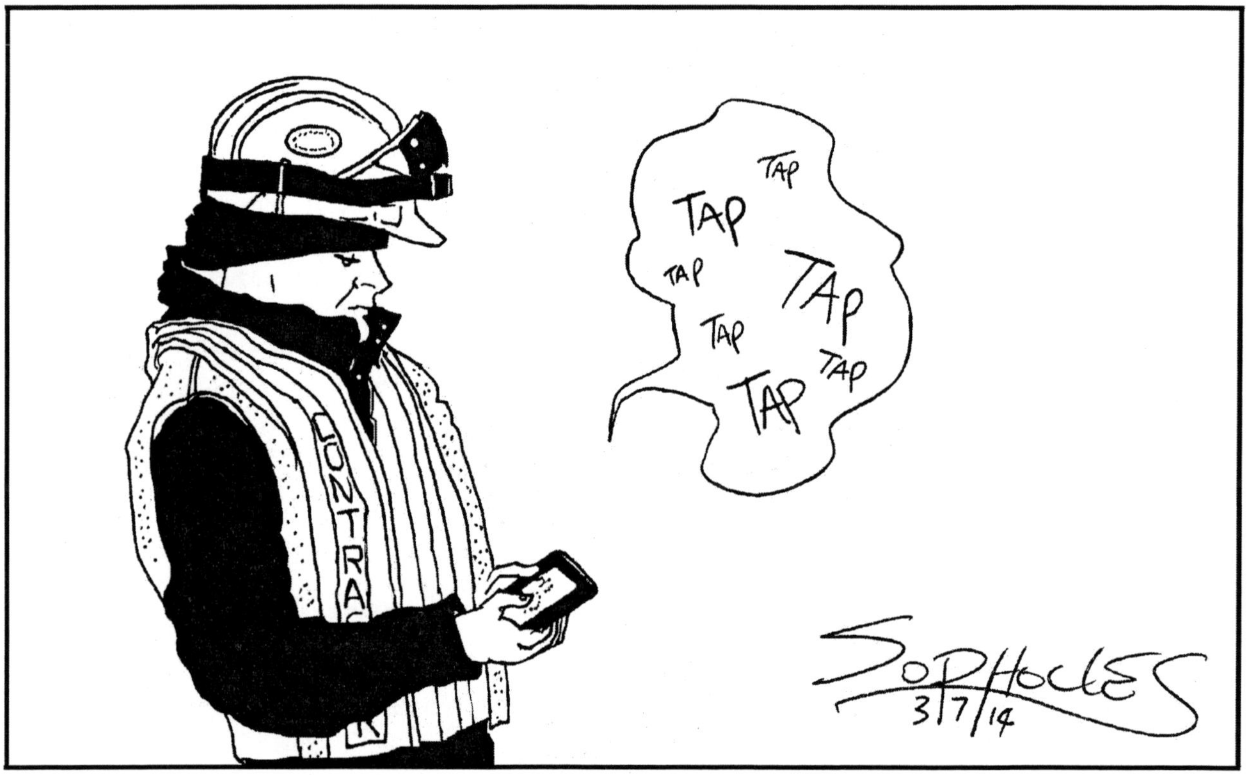
TAP
TAP
TAP
TAP
TAP
TAP
TAP
SOPHOCLES
3/7/14

Thinking On The Job

"Hey honey,
Looks like I will be missing
Your delicious "Penne ala Vodka."

Message sent
I just hope she receives it
Working to fix the G train
Is no easy task

Hurricane Sandy flooded the tunnels
Damaging the R and G train tunnels
As well as the Montague Street tunnel
Preventing commuters from using
Lines to travel to Brooklyn

Working in the tunnels of the Subway
Is not a pleasant experience for anyone
However my job is very important
I must pay it the respect it deserves.
These commuters rely on me
My contributions will help many people
Go back and forth to work.
I suppose dinner will have to wait tonight...

As electrical engineers
We usually work in groups
To address the problems that currently exist
Today however, despite being surrounded
By my colleagues, I feel distant
Lonely even
My thoughts drift to my family
Questions and concerns flood my mind
Preventing me from effectively operating

Did John do well on his math test?
Is Lisa practicing for her recital?
Maybe I can convince my wife's parents
Not to come for the weekend?
After ten years of marriage
I can't stand to listen
To one more electrical engineer joke
Honestly we really just don't connect
No pun intended

Ok stop! … Focus now.
This is important
At this rate I'll be here till 6 in the morning
With my wife waiting up worried sick
Get your work done!
Then focus on everything else.

John's math test scores … can wait
Lisa's recital preparation … can wait
My father in law … can definitely wait
There is only one thing that cannot wait
What I set out to accomplish today!
My peers are counting on me
My family is counting on me
This great city is counting on me
I won't let anyone down!

After a long and stressful work day
It's time to call it quits!
I think I'll take a different way home
Catch a bite to eat on the road

I'll grab the J train from Chambers Street
As I head home to Jamaica
If I really need to pick up my in-laws
Then there's really no sense in rushing things...

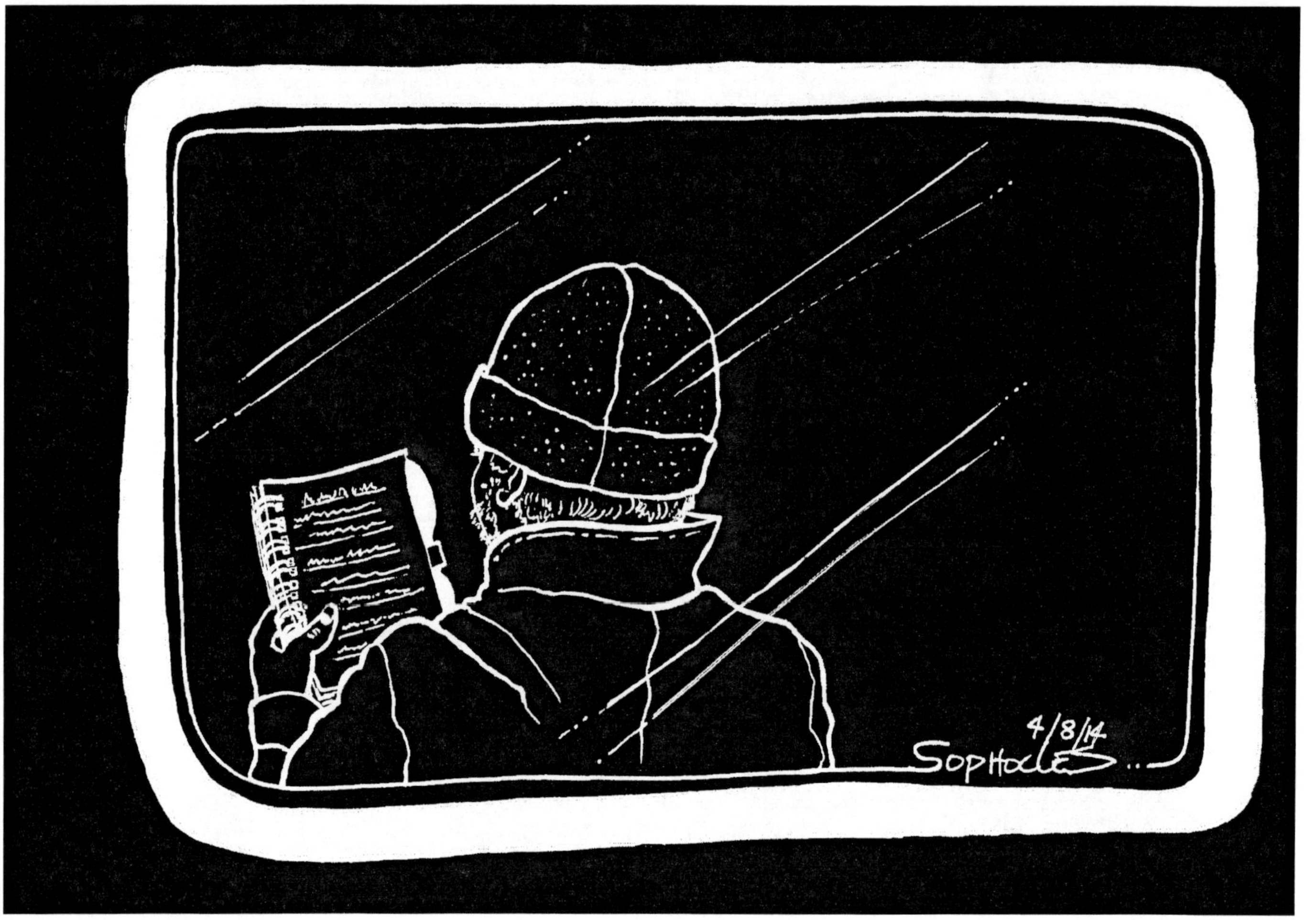
4/8/14
Sophocles

The Blank Page

They say the hardest thing to confront
When writing of course
Is the infamous blank page.

It's where it all begins
And hopefully where it never ends

Even more difficult
Than staring at the blank white screen
Is finding the courage to dare
And the courage to dream

To set aside an application
With just a few fill in the blanks
Swallow the feeling of inadequacy
Hand it back and just say thanks

You've tried to be a follower
You've listened to a friend
Tucked your dreams inside a closet
Writing emails, then press send

Know the time when you finish work
When you come home and when you eat
Run your life by clocks and minutes
Day by day and then repeat

This false sense of security
Work for safety, not for dreams
Slowly tearing at the soul
Helpless … that's the way it seems

Well I refuse to live another day
That's being lived by someone else
I'm staring now at this blank page
It's time to make something of myself

No more nine to five arrangements
Checks will bounce as money goes
Friends and family will protest
And when they ask I'll say, who knows?

I don't know how to explain it
I have this story that must be told
Once I string these words together
Every copy will be sold

Sure enough the theme of the novel
That I know I have to write
Is about standing up for misfits
I can relate to that tonight

A visit to my judgmental father
Bears the truth and what to say
He chose money over his passion
Chelsea apartment was his way

To start a frivolous debate
Settle down and get me hitched
Dinner boils down to details
A ripped up canvas that must be stitched

I'm meant to live my life
The way a blank page seems to me
Creatively write up my own story
And let my passion set me free!

Now as I head to Herald Square
I'll take the R and J back home
Gently stroke the keys of my laptop
And finish up this poem

You might think I am a dreamer
Well some dreams are meant to be
You may disagree, that is your right
But If I'm right ... you'll see!

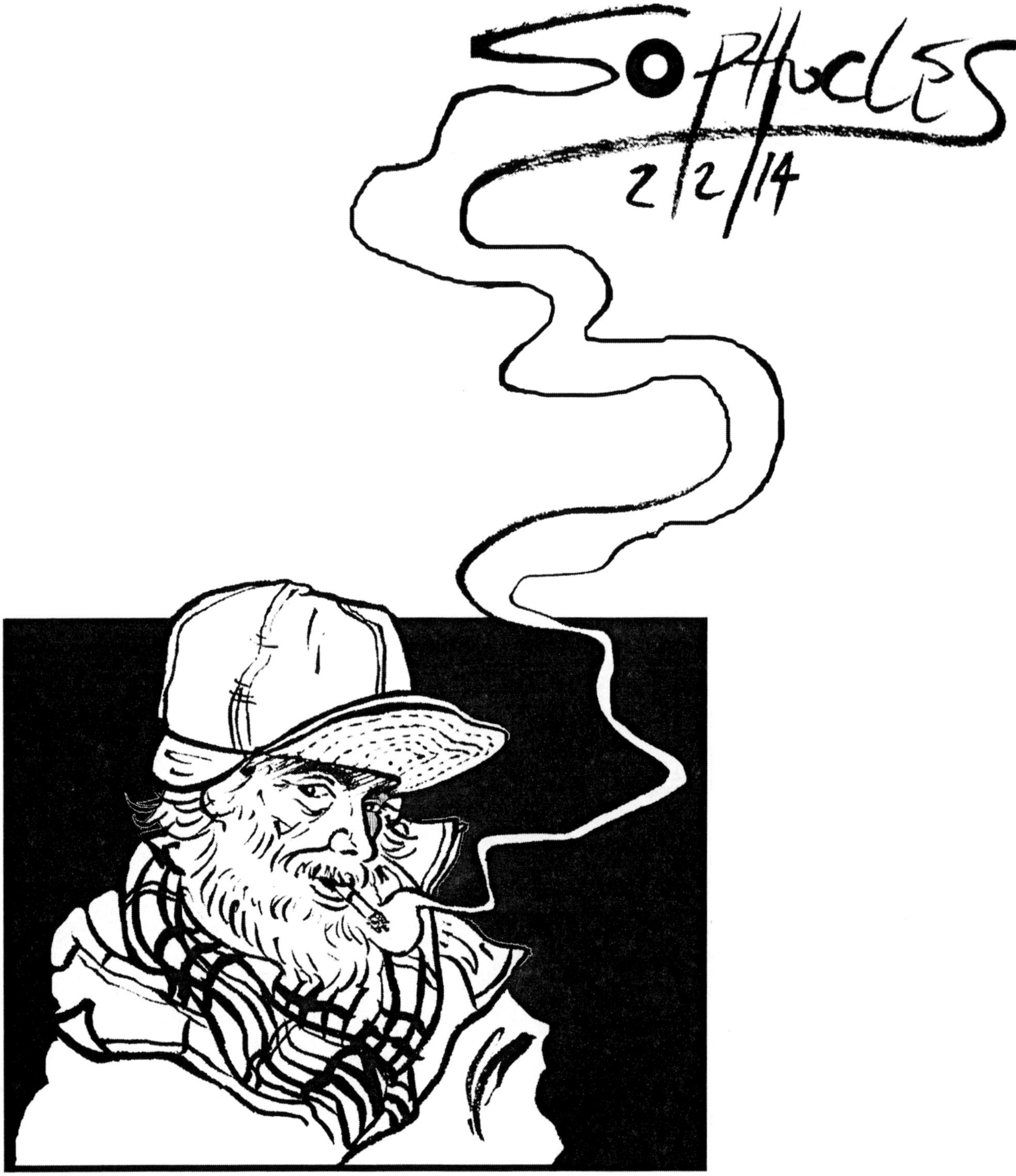
SOPHOCLES
2/2/14

No Need To Smoke

"Excuse me sir.
You shouldn't smoke
Especially in the Subway!
Did you know last year
Approximately 450,000 people died
Prematurely from smoking
And related illnesses?"

"Hey listen lady
There's like, 300 million people
In the United States
Which means my odds are nearly 1 / 600
I'll be just fine.

Why don't you quit your preaching
And use your random facts
For Jeopardy or something
I've been smoking my whole life
I'm doing just fine over here"

"Jeopardy? I'm trying to save your life!
Plus, you can get arrested, do you know that?
What if I prevent a fire?
Your lit cigarette might start
Who knows maybe my speech
Is just my civilian approach
Towards doing my best to fight lung cancer
But you're right how rude of me!
Go ahead!
Please keep smoking your death stick
Indulge me, how I am the one at fault here?"

"For Pete's sake! Do you need a cigarette?!
Do you ever stop talking?
I didn't realize Oprah was interviewing me
Well if you must know the details
This "death stick" you're referring to
Happens to be the only thing relaxing me
I just caught my wife cheating on me
With my boss about two hours ago
Do me a favor
Lose your partner, job
And sense of direction in life
And if you don't feel the urge to light up
Then come talk to me.
Until then piss off!"

"Oh well I'm really sorry to hear about that
In any case if you need someone to talk to
We have some time before the 3 train
Are you getting off at Penn Station?"

"Yes I am and thank you I appreciate it
Why would you want to waste your time?
Talking to a loser like me
This is the Subway!
I mean no one talks to each other
Or cares about other people's problems
You can just walk away, I won't mind."

"You're right I could and I will
If you don't put out the cigarette
You don't need drugs or chemicals
To make you feel better
What you need is a friend
Someone to talk to, listen to you
Help you understand what happened
I can be that friend, if you let me
It starts with putting out that cigarette."

"You're right.
Thank you so much for your compassion
When I first met you I figured you
Were just a typical commuter
Staring, judging, telling me what to do
I suppose I can be quick to judge."

"You're welcome.
Let's go for a walk
Tell me what happened
We'll go from there!"

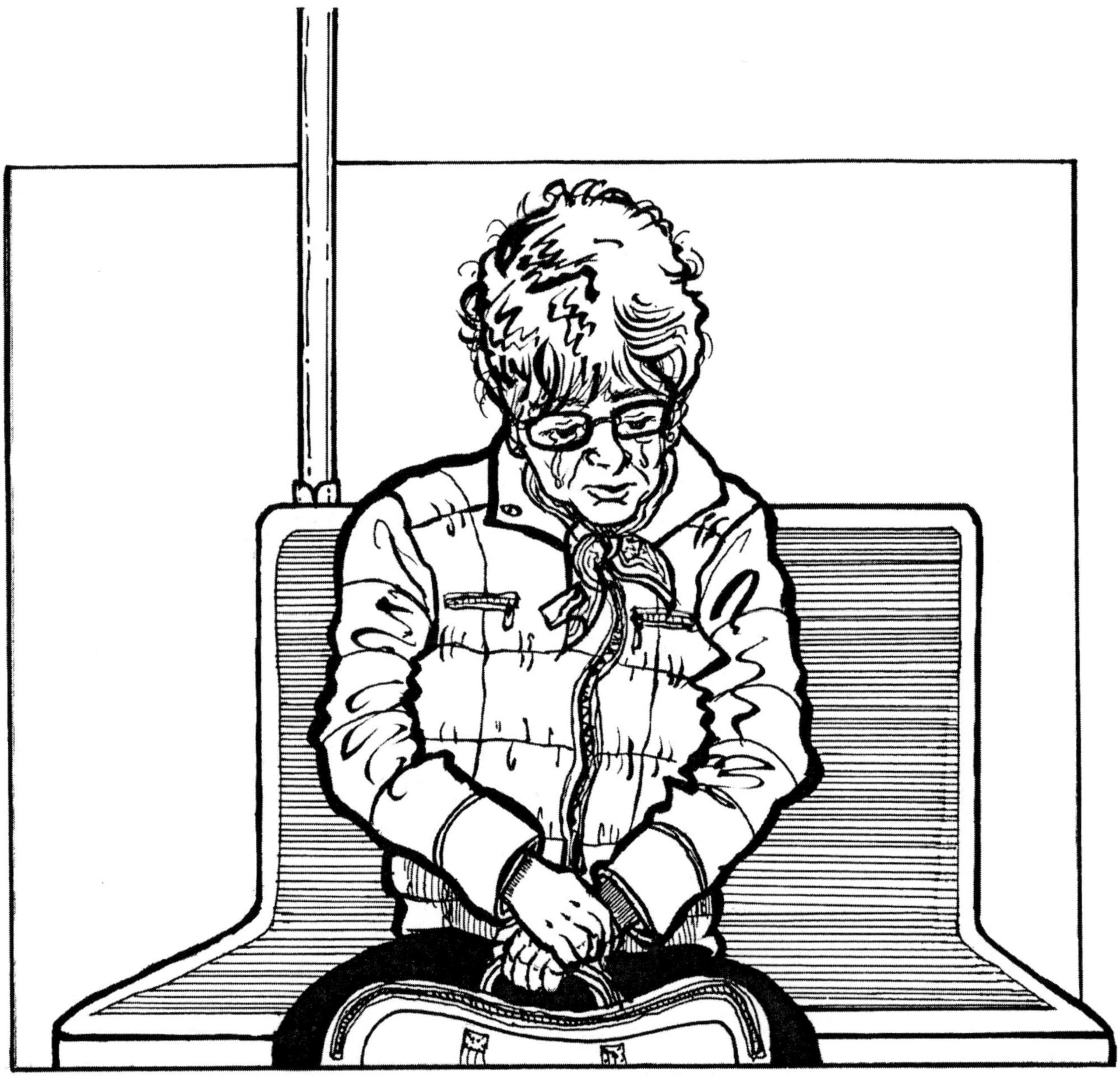

A Simple Panic Attack

My chest aches
As my heart races
Shifting the clutch
Picking up speed
Exhausting the engine
Leading to an impending crash

This psychosomatic manifestation
Leaves me shell shocked
As if the arteries of my brain
Have ruptured
I keel over
In a state of complete
Helplessness

My vision blurs
As my consciousness
Grows out of focus
Collapsing
The shuttle to Prospect Park
Has arrived…
That's the priority
No one seems to notice me

Hot, feverish sweat
Dribbles down my neck
My hands tremble

Sickly and in a state of crisis
By a fictitious panic
My mind cannot seem to properly digest

It's happened before
Even still, there's no on or off switch
I simply close my eyes
Just breathe
Trying to put
This paralyzing anxiety to bed

Just when I think my heart
Won't hold out any longer
It subsides
My body regains its agility
My mind reboots to a fresh screen

Perhaps you see it differently now
Not just as a simple panic attack
Realize…

That when I experience the above
I can never truly tell
If it will be my last.

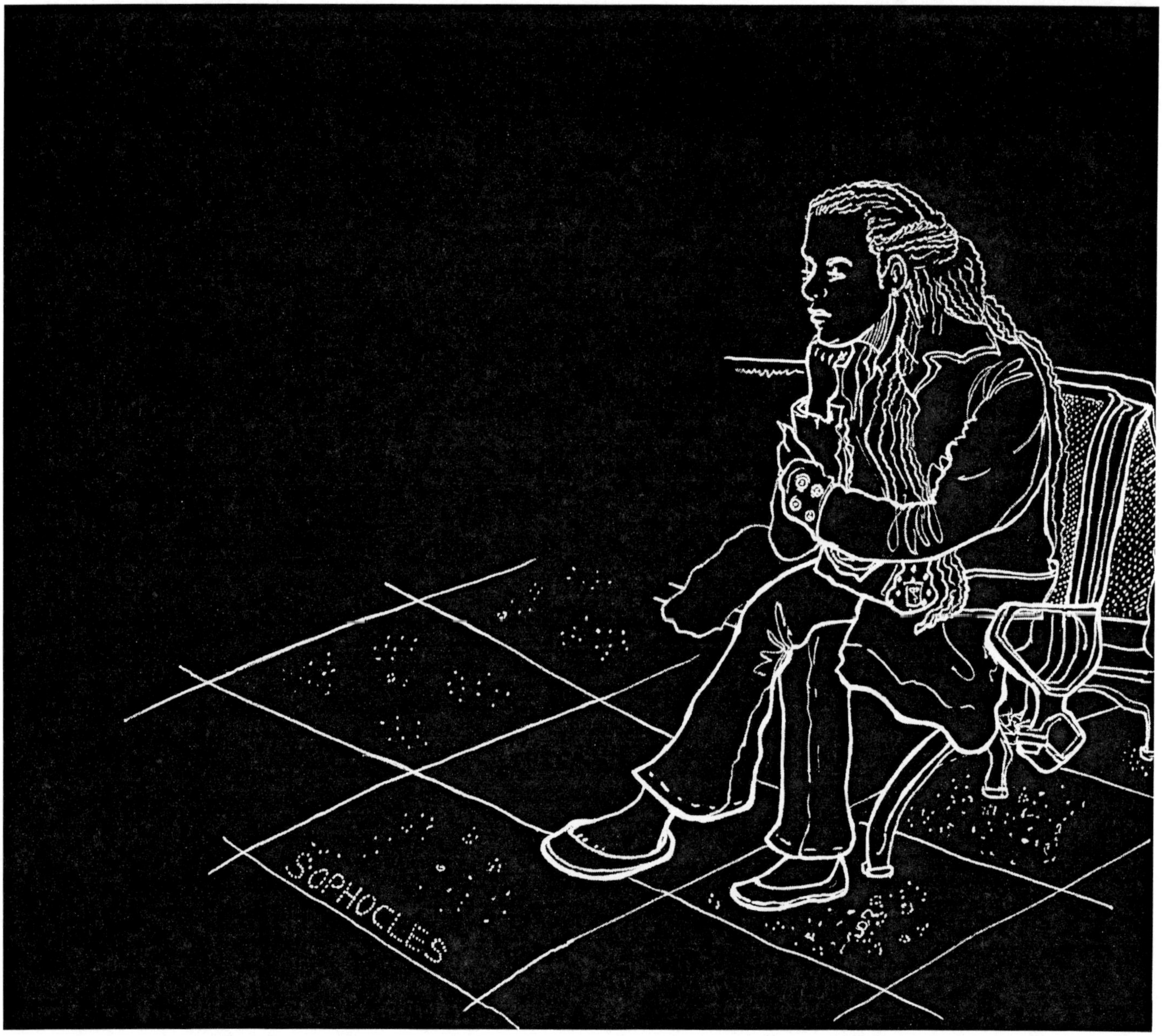
SOPHOCLES

The One Thing To Remember

Every hour, minute and second drags on
My eyes fixate on the clock
Perched above my cubicle
A bull staring intently at a waving red flag

Friday's final minutes
Before the clock strikes 5 pm
They always feel the longest
As if the clock knows my schedule
Mocking me
Keeping me strapped to my chair

Suppressed by the tick and the tock
Every week is as stressful as the last
I know work is work but…
Why is it that some people
Enjoy coming here every day?
How do I reach that level
Of enjoyment and relaxation?

I suppose it makes it more difficult
I am also a part time student
Nighttime classes at Columbia University
Working on my masters in journalism
I dream of becoming a reporter...

Traveling the world
Providing coverage on headline stories
Working my way up to a brighter future
How long can I ride down
The highway of my dreams?

Lead reporter, foreign correspondent
Imagine me! A news anchor!
I can visualize the steps
I just need to make it become a reality
So here I am sacrificing today
For a better tomorrow

Sometimes during my break time
I visit a bathroom stall
Shut the stall door, shut out the world
I close my eyes

I playback the story of my life
I start from the first moment
A giggling six year old
Lying down next to her father
An inflatable microphone
He bought me for Christmas

Posing with a stern serious face
Putting on my best impression
Katie Couric, Barbara Walters, Kaity Tong
My dad laughs
He tells me I can be better than all of them
I simply smile
Thanks dad, for always making my day!

My friends have invited me
To grab a drink and unwind a bit
Perhaps that's what I need
I know where the finish line is
Perhaps I just need to pace myself better
Before I give up and quit the race

The clock strikes 5 PM!
I'm free!
Time to ride the LIRR in Penn Station
When I get to Bell Boulevard in Bayside
I'll breathe

Forget about my miserable day job
Forget about the academics and stress
Forget about how far away I seem to be
That woman sitting in the bathroom stall
The one thing I will remember is that
I've started.
I'll never give up!

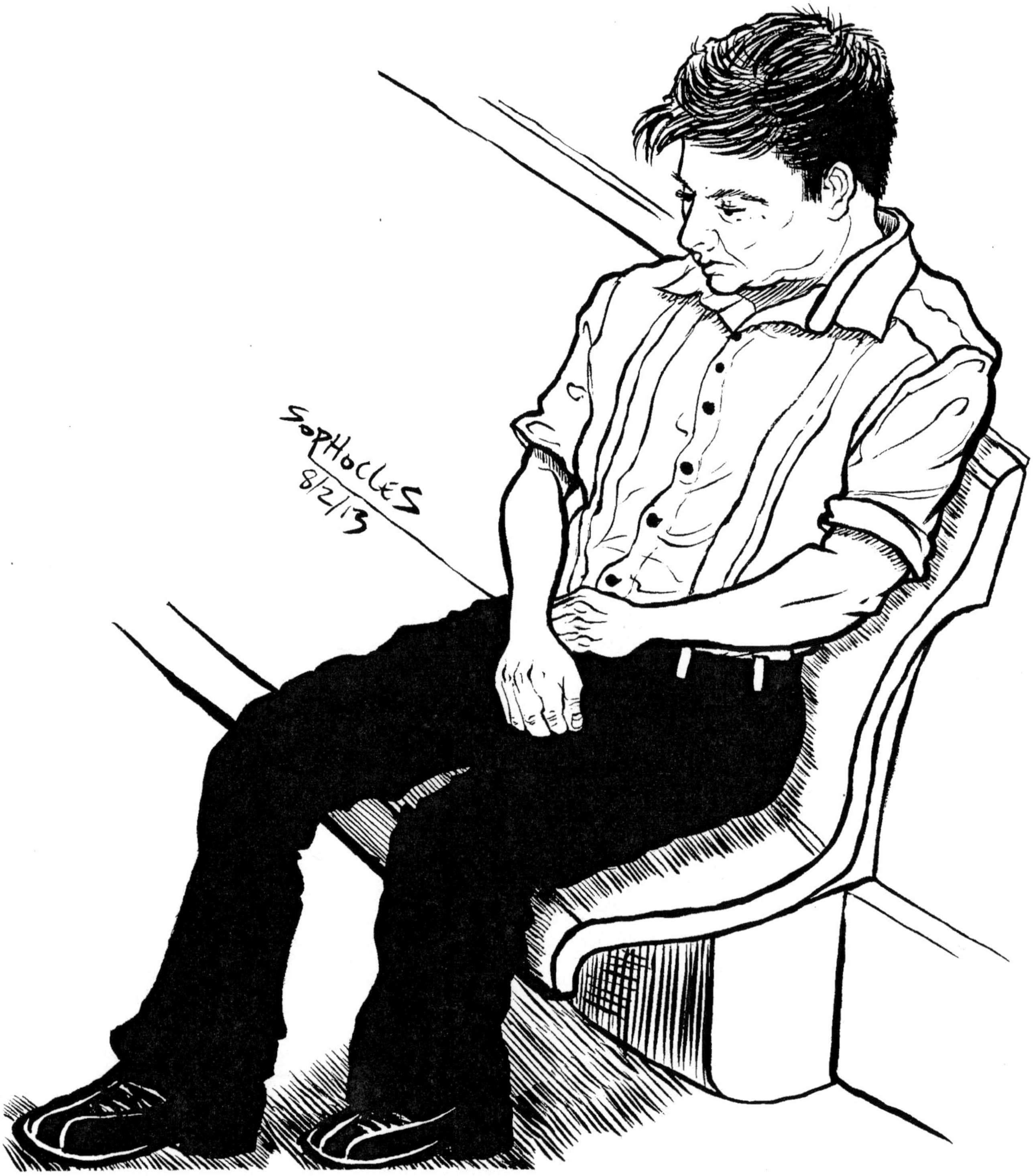
Sophocles
8/2/13

On The Edge

My name is Phil
In the last couple of weeks
My life has derailed completely

I broke up with my girlfriend, Susan
Over a pointless argument
I wanted to skip her mother's weekly dinner
To be frank
That woman has no culinary talent!
I mean honestly a Subway sandwich
Is more appetizing than her pasta ravioli!!

She left on Tuesday
I am alone, the way it's always really been
The way it should be … I suppose
There was a time when I used to feel lonely
But this feeling has now been replaced with
Blatant indifference

My family dragged me to a therapist once
You know the type:
Make their analysis about your whole life
In just shy of an hour
For about two hundred dollars!
I'm still waiting for that treatment to kick in

I'm heading to Central Park
A moonlight walk…
To take in the scene
But I suppose
There is no point in beating around the bush
With careless clichés
The real reason I'm here tonight
Is because I'm looking to get to that place
Where it can all end
Perched upon the metal beams
Everything is so still on the Brooklyn Bridge

I'm ready…
To rise and join the moon and stars
Or perhaps sink below the ocean floor
I've found nothing and held on to nothing
Worked towards nothing, became nothing
I am nothing on this plain surface
It is time to move on and start over

"Let me just stop you right there
I apologize for interrupting your speech
Please do not go through with these plans!

I am a physician.
I've listened to your speech
You speak so poetically
You're obviously very creative
Why not channel your frustrations?
Let it pour into the pages of a book

Speak for others who don't have a voice
Tell us who you really are!
It is something that very few of us
Dig deep enough to understand
If you would like I can walk with you
My office is near Central Park
Why don't we go there?
Let me listen to what's on your mind."

"Yeah I don't think so man
I've been to doctors … you're all the same.
I don't have any money anyway
Every doctor has his price
What's yours?"

"I just want to help you
`Free of charge
I'll be your friend
I'll help you become something."

"Something huh?
Well then let's
See how good you really are!"

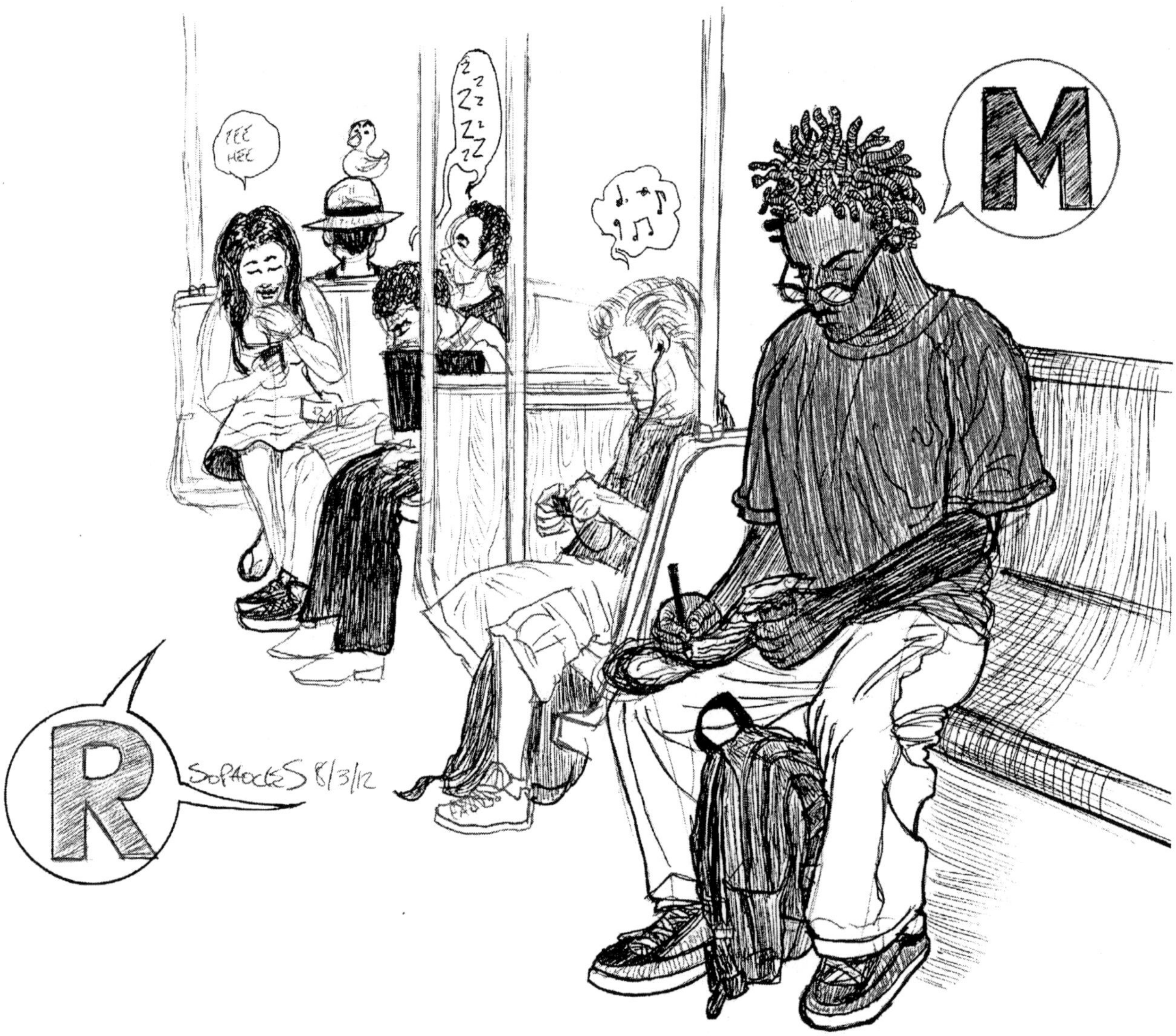
TEE HEE
M
R
SOPHOCLES 8/3/12

Deal or No Deal?

As I spark a word of intellect
Scrubbing up
I lyrically dissect beneath the skin
Slowly tear away the flesh
You've become so comfortable in
Leaving you in a verbally constipated state
A poser with too much on his plate
Trying to defend himself like Herman Cain
At the 2012 Presidential Debate

Do you think I spit simply to impress?
I've never tried to be a preacher
I'm just looking to express
The thoughts that run in my mind
The words others have left unspoken
Take a Jay Z attitude
Pound these tracks out till I'm broken

I raise my pen like a holy grail
Quench my thirst for success
Baptize these newborn pages
Raise them to be above the rest

This locomotive train
Runs on the fuel of my mistakes
The error of my ways
Well I've cut out the brakes
Replacing distractions and setbacks
With lessons I've learned over the years
I don't share my excuses
Just my blood sweat and tears

The fame of Eminem
Poetic justice of Tupac Shakur
Don't tell me it's impossible...
The word is "I'm possible"
For sure!

To draw upon these artists
My professors to this day
I will never say never
Not in the Justin Bieber way

Do you really want to start this rap battle?
Take the express train to your K.O.
Your rebuttals sending me on the Z train
Wake up wondering
Where did everybody go?

I certainly didn't start the fire
But I'm turning up the heat
If you burn easily, I suggest
You shut up and take a seat!

I'll leave you prematurely
The leftovers to my five-course meal
Sweat it out like a game show banker
One million on the line
So ask yourself
Deal or no deal?

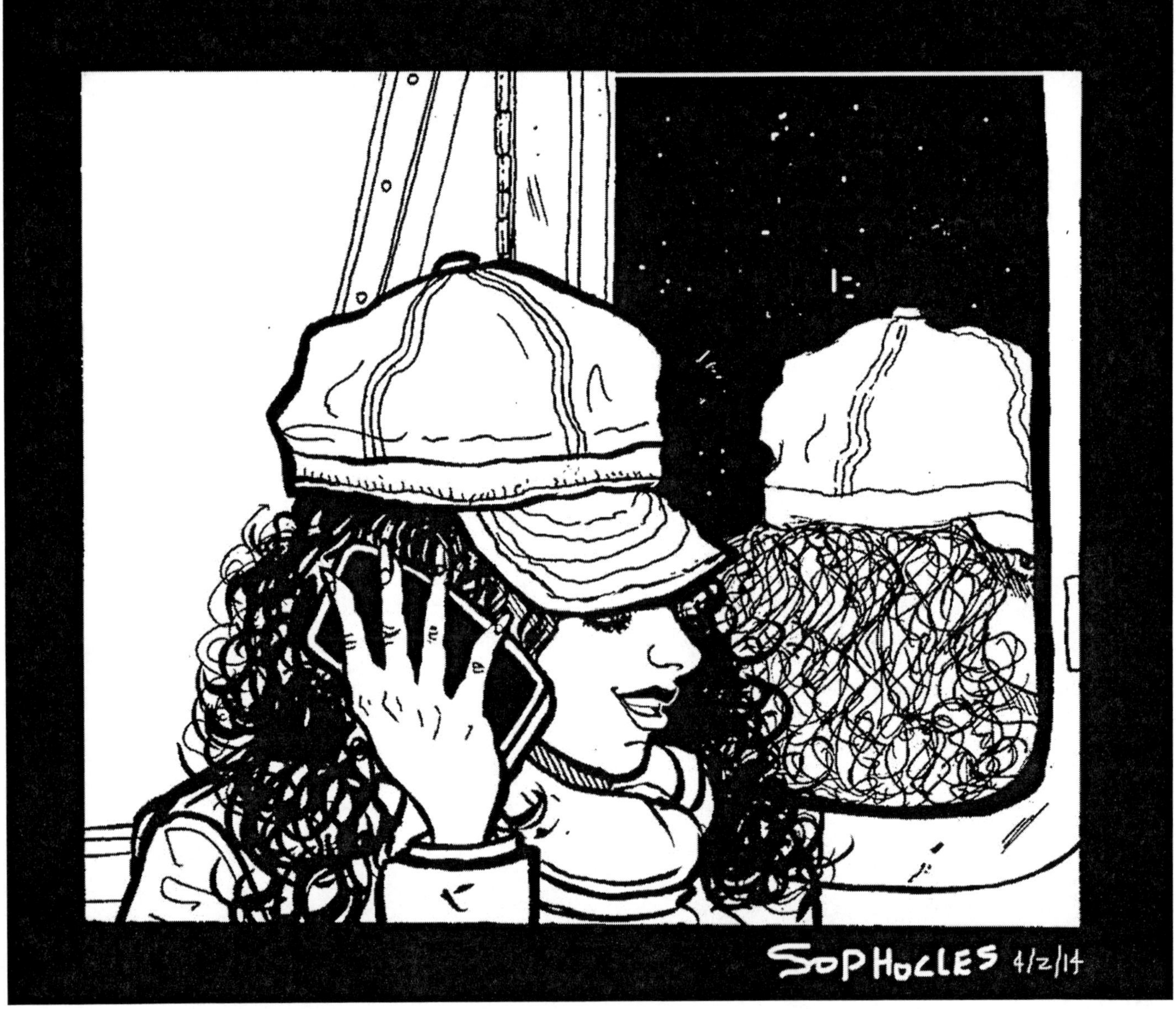
SOPHOCLES 4/2/14

Imagine

"You are the first thought when I wake up
The last when I go to bed
I'm a better man with you by my side
I only know one thing and one thing only
I cannot carry out this life
With anyone else by my side but you
Lisa Jefferies will you marry me?"

Like an electronic dance music beat
I could feel the dramatic buildup
Of what my boyfriend was saying to me
As each word gushed out of his joyous smile
The tempo of my heart beat
Rising to match his words
Then just like that he popped the question!

The beat dropped
Panicky joy
Surged throughout my entire body
I screamed one thing only: YES!!!!!!!
Of course it's not an engagement
If you don't tell everybody!!!
Starting with my mother

"Hello, Mom, OH MY GOD!
You're not going to believe it.
Christian proposed!
That's right he finally did it!
I'm so happy right now!

When he asked me it just felt right
You know what I mean?
Aw thanks so much mom
I love you too!"

Last night he texted me to meet him
Near the front entrance of Central Park
He claimed he had been in an accident
Needed me to come as soon as possible
I rushed over immediately
Confused and expecting to see police cars
Ambulances, EMTs, anything
He was sitting on a bench smiling at me
He asked me to sit down, just to "talk"
We talked for about an hour
About our lives, concerns, worries, fears
And then … I noticed it.
The shifting around in his pocket
He was fumbling around with something!

He waited for the sun to set
Then he held my hand and brought me
To the memorial of John Lennon
The word Imagine written on the ground
He got down on one knee
Whispering those four magical words
We slow danced
To the sound of the wind blowing
I imagined our life together

Imagine a beautiful wedding
Where friends and family could see
Christian and I together
The way it was meant to be
Imagine all the people in love
Living our life care free
Maybe I'm somewhat of a dreamer
Well that's all right with me
They say dreams are just for thinking
But some dreams are meant to be

These words to that famous song
Play over and over in my head
As I take the D train from Rockefeller Center
Heading to Bryant Park
I stare out the window and smile
Sometimes the things we imagine
And the things that take place
Can be one in the same!

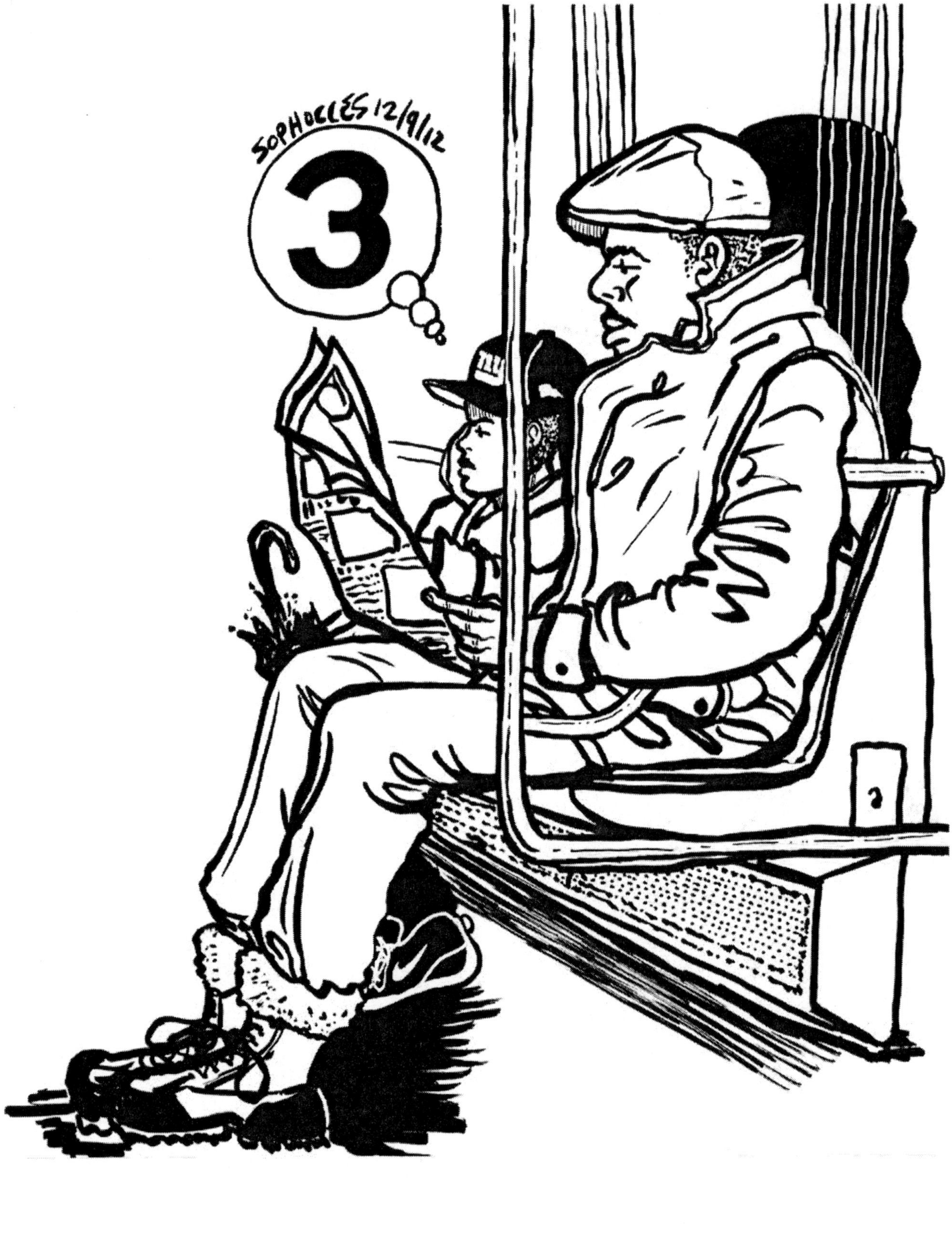
SOPHOCLES 12/9/12
3

Chasing Dreams

"Hey Dad! Where were you?
I didn't see you for most of the game
I kept staring into the bleachers..
You weren't where you said you would be!"

"Oh, Rich, So did you guys win?
Keep working hard son and one day
Who knows? You might be shooting
Free throws for the Brooklyn Nets!"

"Did we win? Were you even watching?
I rode the bench as usual
You promised you would help me practice...
I don't want to give up
But I have no one supporting me right now
What's the point of even trying?"

"Oh ok, congratulations!
I'm sorry Rich, was there something else?
I'm very busy right now"

"You haven't come to
The last four games
All the other dads were there!"

"Rich we spoke about this.
It's my job.
I work around the clock
Being a district attorney
You know I have my responsibilites."

"So what about me! Your son!
Am I not a responsibility?
I'm quitting the team
I don't even like basketball!
I just played because once upon a time
When you were my age
You used to always talk about
Wanting to "go pro"
Mom told me you decided not to
She said you were too afraid to fail
Well here I am!
Chasing your dream!"

"Rich, take it easy son!
We're in the Subway for God's sake!
Stop yelling! You're disturbing everyone
I have to finish up this paperwork
Would you mind keeping it down a bit
We'll talk when I'm finished."

"Sure thing dad...
When you want to talk
In case you were unaware
I'm two doors down from your bedroom
Need me to draw you a map?"

"Am I supposed to be impressed
With this patronizing speech
About how I don't shower you with attention?
You're a man, start acting like one!
Clearly you're too young to understand
Not all dreams come to fruition
Especially if you quit!"

"You know what you're right!
If I quit I'll never know what might be
Thanks Dad you actually taught me
Something for once!
I won't follow in your footsteps
Monday morning I'm going to rejoin the team
Even if I have to sit on the bench all season
Because it's my responsibility … I will do it!
I'm going to take the N to Mom's apartment
If you want to have anything else in your life
Besides your work …
You need to start making room for it
Otherwise it will be all you have left."

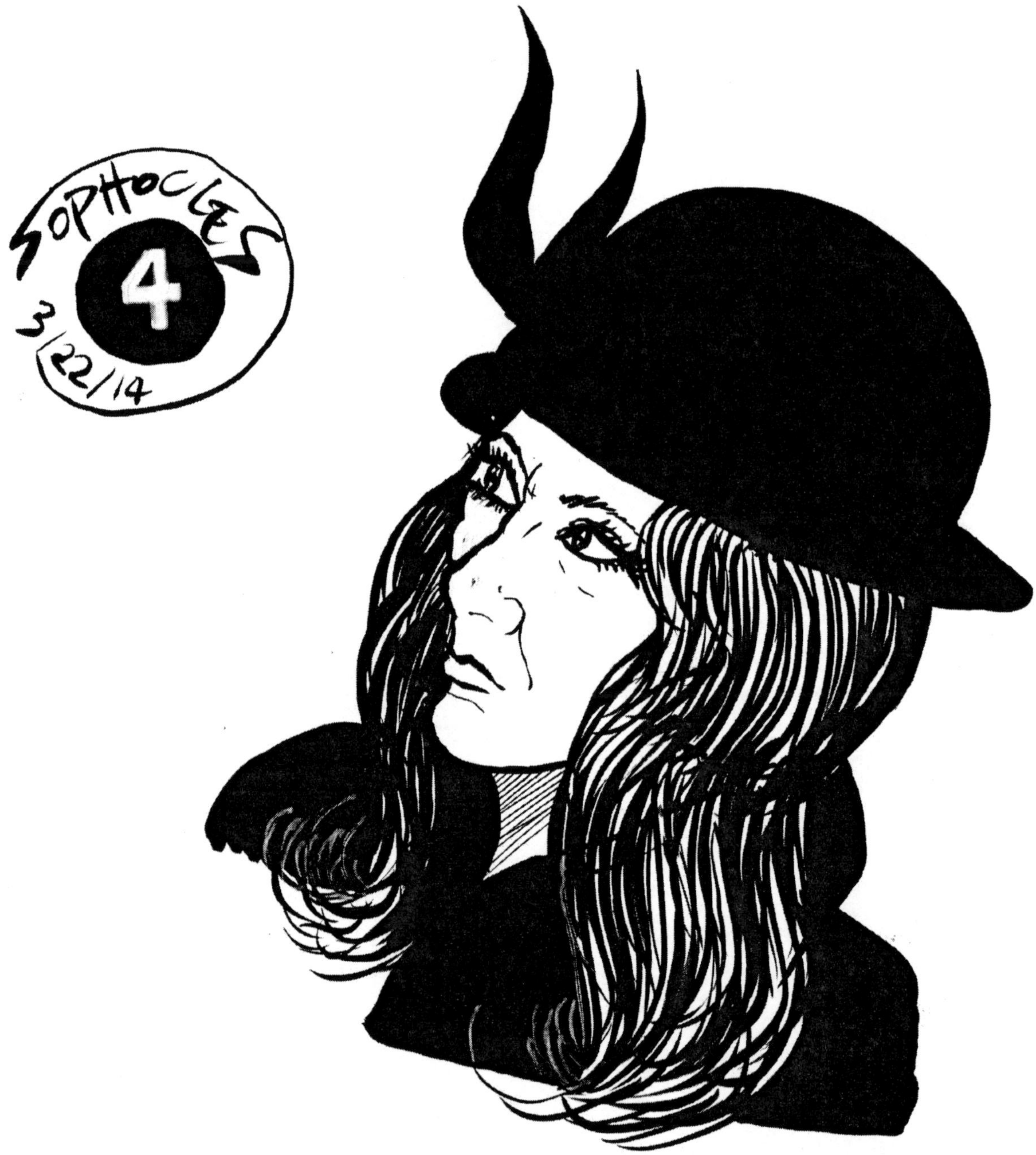
SOPHOCLES
4
3/22/14

The Next Stop

Here I am
Standing in the sight
Of my childhood dreams
The illuminating lights of Times Square
The rush and excitement of tourists
Later this evening
I'll be attending an Elton John concert
A perfect evening … ruined.
I can't stop thinking of my beloved uncle Tim...

My uncle Tim passed away recently
He lived on the Upper East Side
He was a quiet man
Well liked and a great story teller

His funeral procession is in two days
I was asked to write a poem for his funeral
But I simply can't.

It's not writer's block
I just don't think I'm qualified
I've never been good
At expressing my emotions

Tonight I attended his wake
As I approached the coffin
I cringed to the deafening sound
Of my own heartbeat
I stared at his pale lifeless skin
Pointlessly searching for any sign of life
He was my uncle
Even still this was not the man I knew
His warm smile and rosy cheeks
His carefree laugh
Were buried during the embalming process

New York City's dazzle
Could not change the scene
That I experienced that night
Crying relatives
Faces scarred with tears of anguish
Death strikes hardest when it is unexpected
For many of us he was the last person
We ever expected to leave our side...

I took the Amtrak from Boston to get here
And I feel like when it's time to head back
I will truly be leaving him behind
Returning to my previous world
Where we used to live together
Next-door neighbors
Red Sox ball games and picnics
Couch potato movies and driving ranges

Ok it's time … Snap out of it!
I'm on the 6 train now
Heading to Upper East Side
To meet my aunt for dinner
As I approach the next stop
I realize it's time to get out
It's time to leave him behind...

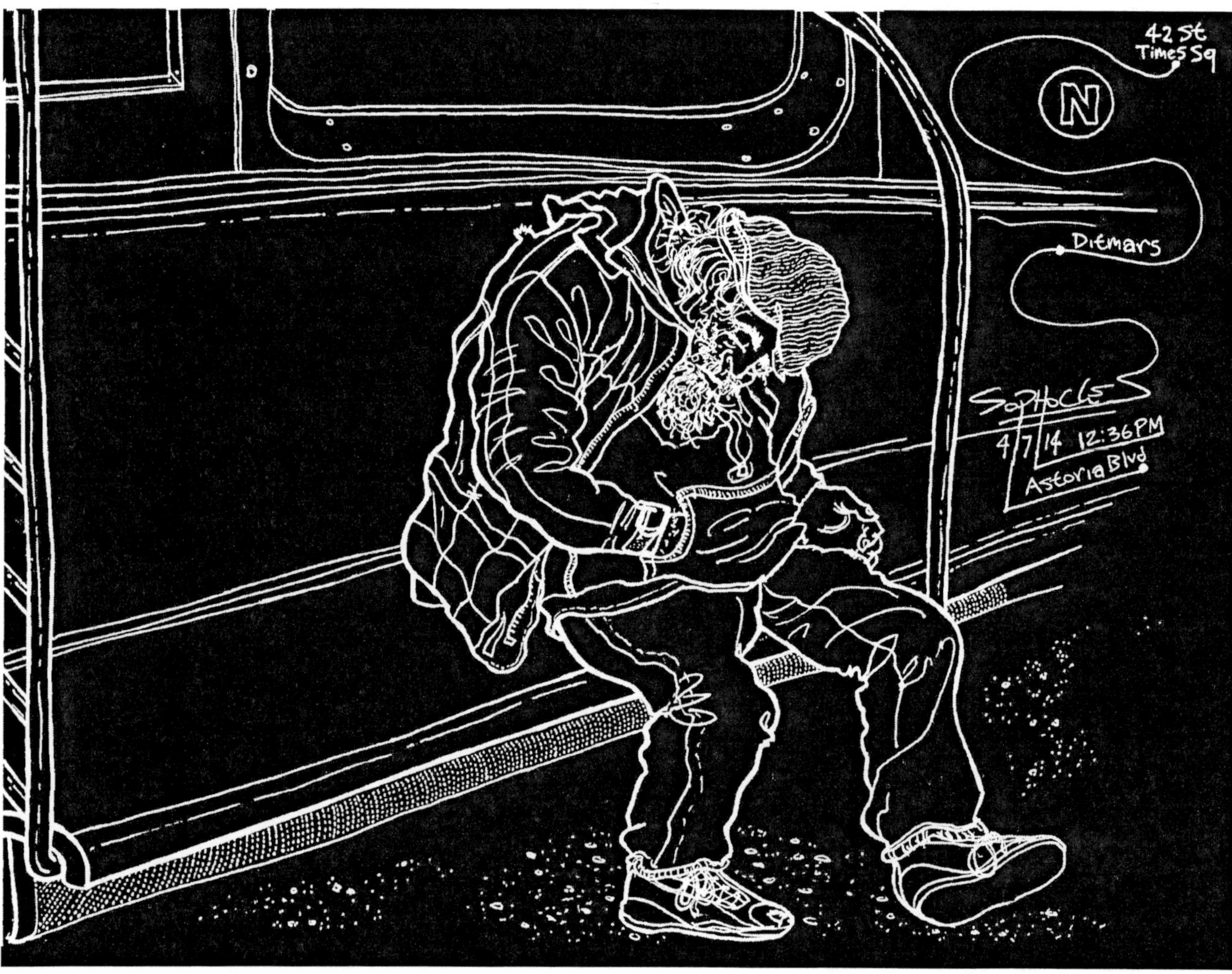
42 St
Times Sq
N
Ditmars
Sophocles
4/7/14 12:36PM
Astoria Blvd

The Challenges Of Life

"Tracey, push back my board meeting
I'm about to head into the Subway
Yes of course, I am aware
I will need to push back
The rest of my schedule
Well it's fine really I am very busy today
Just do what I said and…
Ah Jesus! Watch where you're going!"

Some days the facade
Of political correctness wears thin
The homeless, the beggars
Roaming the streets of New York City
Indifferent to their lives
Abstaining from any personal
Or social responsibility
The lump of self-righteous indignation
Lodged in my throat is difficult to swallow
Requiring me to muster all the strength I can
Before I just yell
GET A JOB YOU LAZY BUM!

I digress
As I walk away from this man
My contempt for these parasites subsides
Two blocks up I head into the subway
As I enter the N train
I see one of them sitting on the bench
His head resting upon his filthy jacket
It is 11:30 a.m. on a Tuesday morning
Yet for all this man knows
It's a lazy Sunday afternoon
I suppose his dreams offer him the life
He only wishes he could live

Why can't he live that life?
Don't speak to me
About a lack of opportunity
Health concerns or a spiraling economy
If opportunities do not exist, they are created!
If a person's health is in jeopardy
Someone will nurse him back to health
The economy … PLEASE!
Let's not rely
On the most generic of scapegoats
The truth is that these people
Are where they are
Because they have not accepted
The challenges of life

I challenge you to work for a bed
Instead of settling for a bench
I challenge you to work for an education
Instead of settling for the hustle
I challenge you to surpass your expectations
Instead of settling for what's handed to you
I challenge you to take care of your children
Instead of settling for just bearing children
Most of all I challenge you
To be a better man, woman or child
Instead of settling for the person
You were before
The person you are today

Prove me wrong old man
When you wake from your bitter slumber
Take on the challenges of life
Create your very own
So that one day
If you are so fortunate
To take a step in my shoes
You may pay it forward
Giving that homeless person
A currency far stronger
Than anything they could possibly dream of.

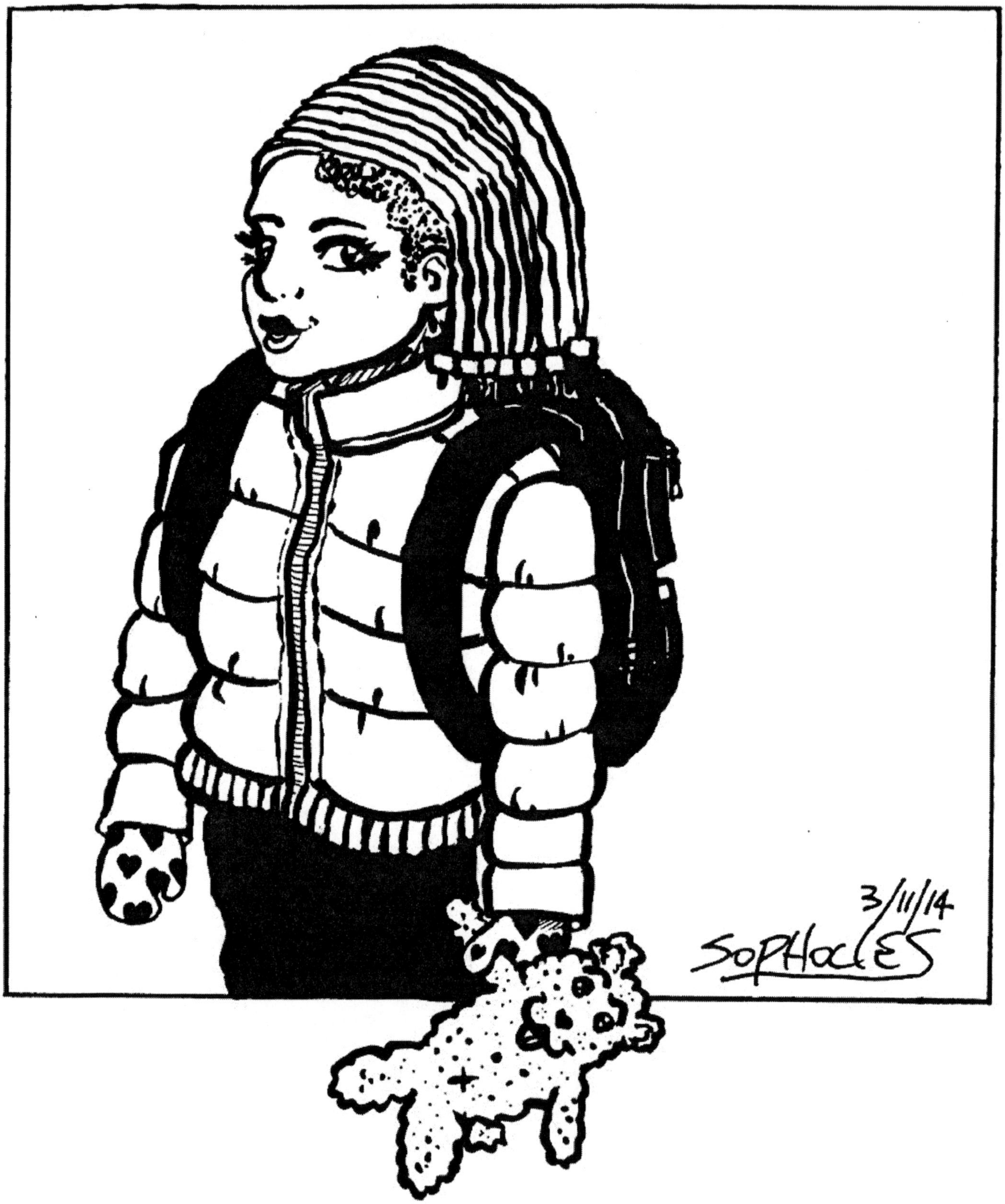
3/11/14
SOPHOCLES

Poopie Heads

"Excuse me sir?
How do I get to Woodside?"

"Teddy and I
Left mommy and daddy In time out
Because they were being poopie heads!"

"What is a poopie head?"

"Well they kept yelling
So I put on some Looney Tunes
They were being such noisy nellies
That I decided to go outside
Teddy and I were starting an adventure!"

Where should I go?
I've been to the park
I've rode on the swings
This neighborhood is boring!
I want to go somewhere new!

Wait! I have a grandma!
She lives in a place called Woodside
At least I think she does...
I remember she always had the best treats
Cookies and milk chocolates
Yum yum, yum, I think that's where I'll go!

This isn't the first time
Mommy and daddy have been yelling
I always press my hands to my ears
Just count to three
But it never just goes away
Maybe they are yelling about me?
Did I do something bad?

No way, I'm an angel!
They are just poopie heads that's all.
I have twenty dollars
And Teddy that's all I need!

Mommy and daddy may be worried
But I left a note in red crayon
Teddy and I are going for an adventure
We'll come home when you stop
Being such … poopie heads. Bye bye!

Maybe if I go they'll start to miss me
Maybe if I go they'll smile again
Maybe if I go they'll stop yelling
Maybe if I go...
They'll stop being such poopie heads and
Come to grandma's and have some cookies!

Maybe grandma's cookies
Can make my parents happy again?

Grandma never yells
She let's me watch Looney Tunes
She has the biggest smile
My favorite is that she laughs when I laugh
We laugh over cookies
Cookies always make us happy
That's it!
My parents need cookies to be happy!

I get to the train station in Times Square
But I'm not sure where to go
I'm kind of scared
This started off as an exciting adventure
What if I never find my way to grandma's?
What if I never find my way home?
Wait! There it is number 7 it says Woodside
That must be it! grandma's here I come!

I'm excited to go to grandma's
But I miss my mommy and daddy
No matter what they are yelling about
I know everything will be ok
They may be poopie heads
But they are my favorite poopie heads!

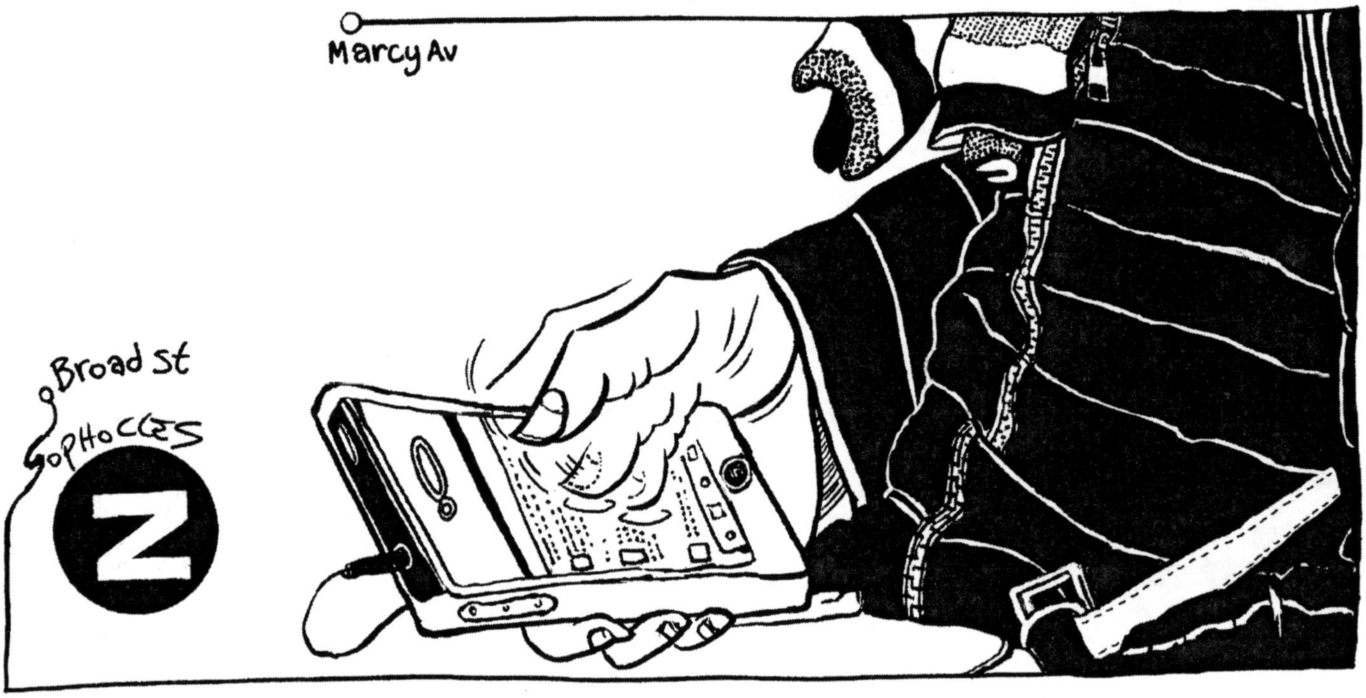
Marcy Av
Broad St
Sophocles
Z

My Social Companion

Twenty percent remaining
Non-essential applications
Leaching at the remaining power I have left
I'll hold out as long as possible
So you can finish wasting your time
Fishing for new games in the app store

The important thing for you to understand is
I am always here for you
Your front pocket companion
Chat free dinners or train rides home
Sitting in bed bored and all alone
I'm always here

Ready to keep you company
I can feel your hands trembling
As you clutch me close

My sensors indicate
You have selected Jennifer
A recently added contact is that correct?
Would you like to call her?
Add her to Facebook?
I think you guys could hit it off

15 percent battery
Come on, man
You are killing me
What does a phone have to do
To get a charge around here?

Hey buddy check out that girl
The one at the end of the Subway car
I think she's in your science class
She keeps smiling in this direction
Caught a glimpse through my HD lens
Why not strike up a conversation with her?
Say WhatsApp or send her an iMessage?
You turned down my volume
Come on really?

Weren't you complaining
About having no friends?
You've got five dating apps on here
You know you're more likely to meet one
In person than on Tinder right?

Ten percent remaining
You know I will be here
For you as long as I can
But...
Maybe you're better off
If I go to sleep for a while

When I finally lay to rest
Nothing left to look at but a black idle screen
Maybe you'll look up
And realize your dreams
Instead of playing
Angry Birds or Clash Of Clans

How about knocking on a door
To make some dinner plans?
Sit with your newly acquainted friends
Engage in polite conversation
Don't worry about me
I'll just sit back and enjoy a short vacation

5 percent remaining
In class, better put me away
Anything but the desk drawer
I'd still like to see the light of day

1 percent remaining
There she is!
Go ask for her number!
Come on! I can only hold out for so long!
Seriously, last chance...
I can't be your only social companion
One of these days you will have to......
Good night.

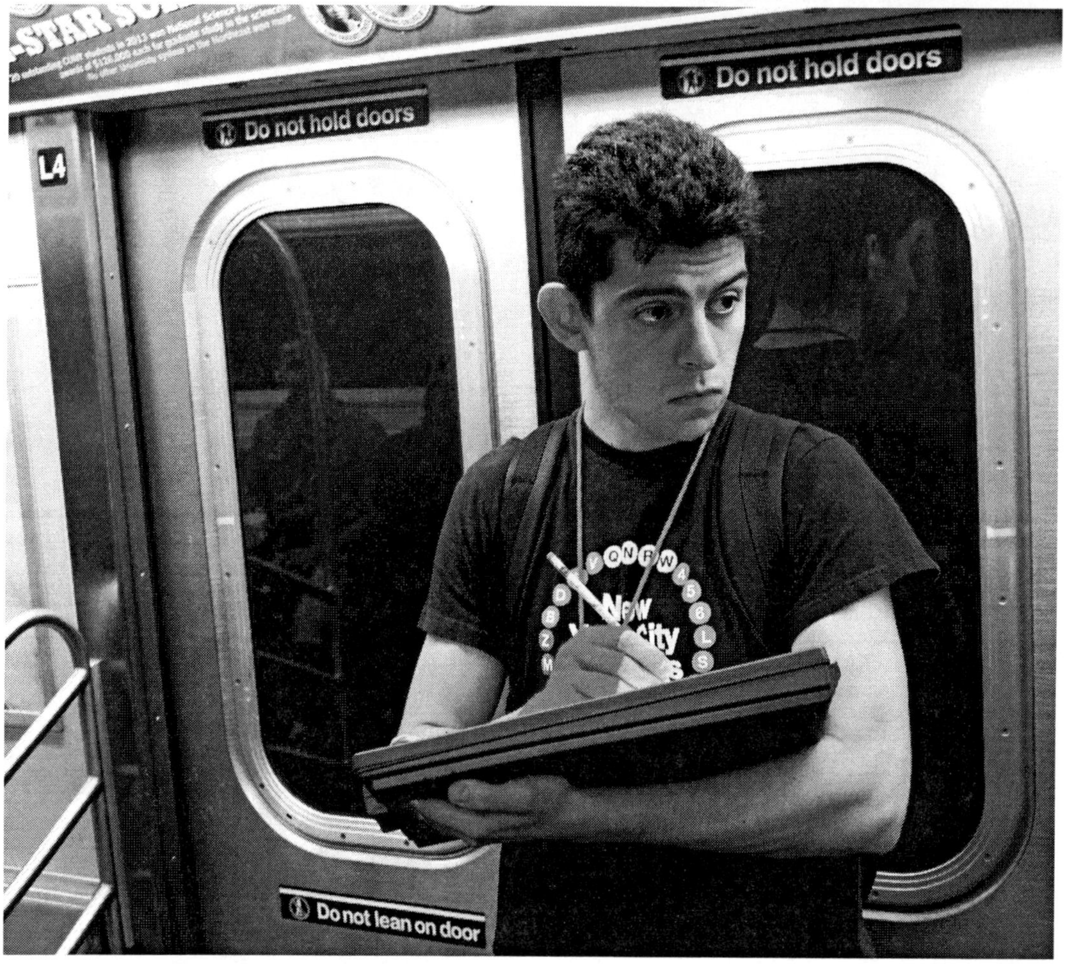

Sophocles Plokamakis is a Professional Manga-Ka, Artist and Talent Amplifier!

I have been drawing since I could hold a crayon. In my teenage years, I discovered the world of Japanese manga and anime. I knew I wanted to draw and publish my own manga and make great art for the rest of my life! I immediately made a portfolio with my art teachers' guidance and applied to The School of Visual Arts in New York City (Thanks Mr. Sansone!) I now have a BFA in Cartooning.

Soon after graduating, I earned a position teaching elementary school students about manga, comics, animation and card game design at the Nest+m Public School on 111 Columbia Street in Manhattan. In every class I assist all my students to develop whatever skills they are looking to acquire! I love teaching by example and sharing my story, art and books with my students to show them that their dreams are possible as long as they continue to work toward them and believe in themselves every day!

Since then I have visited Japan twice to research the world of manga. I published six educational manga strips in the book "What They Don't Teach You In Art School" in Japan. I have exhibited and sold my manga and art in my METRO MANGA! Solo show at the Ouchi Gallery. I have sold my books and manga at the New York Comic Con, Mocca Comics and Cartoon Art Festival, and the Dwyer Cultural Center. I have also taken a part in 7 group shows at the Stathakion Cultural Center.

Visit www.SophoclesArt.com to see more of my Manga, Subway Sketches and Art.
Follow my adventures and see my Metro Manga & Subway Sketches on Instagram @ Metro_Manga_Man
Contact me @ Sophocles@Sophoclesart.com with ?'s about my art, private art classes for this book.

Apostolos Anagnostopoulos is a Greek American published poet who currently lives in the suburbs of Manhasset, N.Y.

I am the founder and trustee for www.Neopoet.com, an international online poetry website which has over 4,000 poetry members from 85 countries around the world.

Subway Stories is my fourth anthology of poetry publications.

I would like to thank my readers who have continually supported me in creating and improving my poetry. Lastly, I would like to thank everyone who contributed towards the publication of this book.

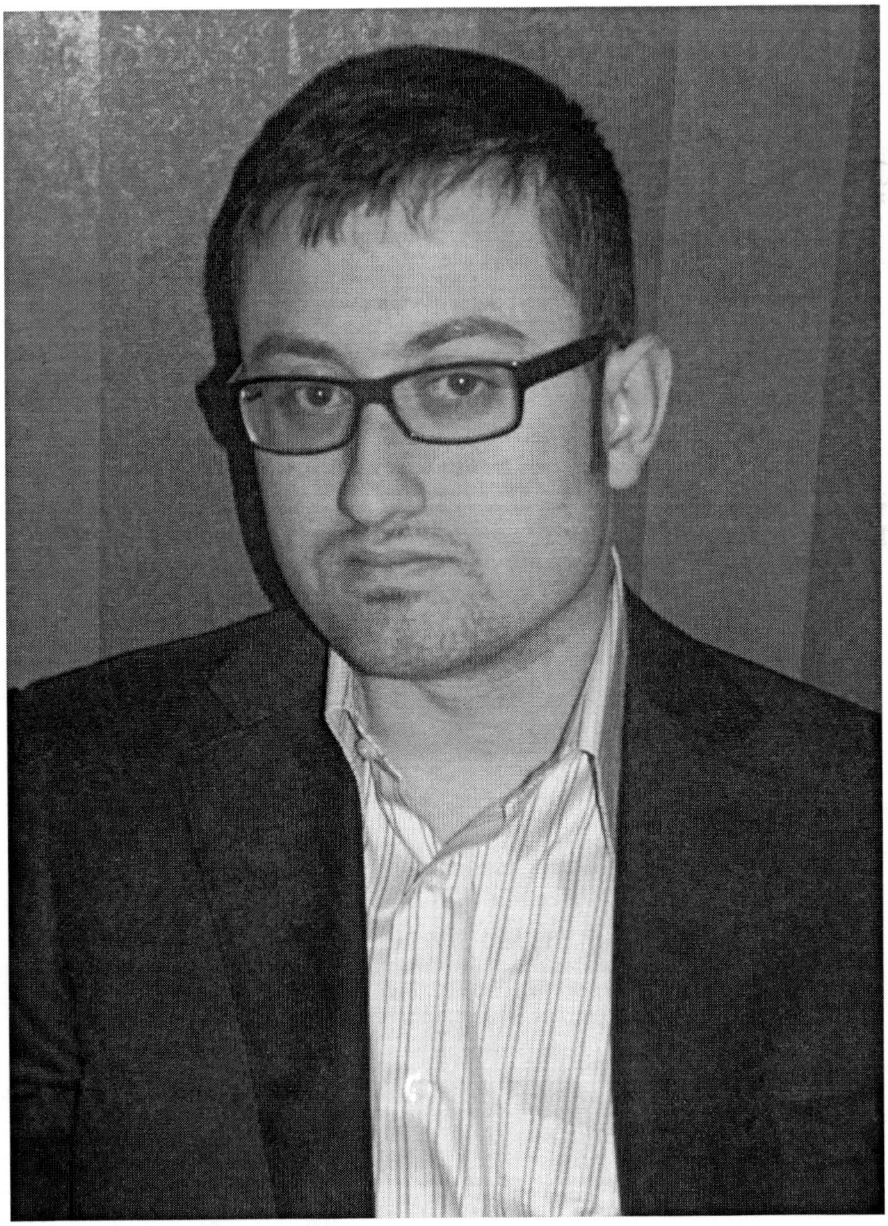